"Richard Irwin shows us that one doesn't need mind-numbing jargon to write a powerful, challenging, and compelling book on following Jesus in our chaotic and hazardous world. It is many things braided together—a sustained engagement with Jeremiah, a series of sermons and pastoral reflections, and profound personal testimony. As a veteran pastor and a serious student of scripture and the world, Irwin does so much of importance in relatively few pages. Be good to yourself and your friends and take time to sit with Irwin's humble-yet-courageous gift to the church."

—Michael L. Budde
Professor of Political Science and Catholic Studies, DePaul University

"Forget the 'nice book,' this is a theological punch in the gut. Through the fierce, faithful lens of the prophet Jeremiah, Irwin delivers a timely and unsettling confrontation for the American Church. Supported by powerhouse scholars, he precisely exegetes Scripture to draw incisive parallels between Judah's fall and the church's precarious witness. This essential work tackles the central question: What does faithful leadership look like when everything is falling apart? It doesn't sugarcoat. It tells the truth loud, clear, and costly, and dares you to hope anyway."

—Stephen Cheyney
Minister, Niner United, University of North Carolina Charlotte

"Part essay, part commentary on Jeremiah, part sermon—Irwin lays out the challenges facing the church in the United States in this 'time of profound loss.' Through it all, his pastoral heart and love of the church shine bright as he calls us to a 'more faithful, cross-carrying way,' and to 'live out the story of hope' in these times."

—Victor Hinojosa
Associate Professor of Political Science, Baylor University

"Pastor Irwin is an unlikely Jeremiah. He lives in the foothills of Western North Carolina and could take refuge there in an easy path to being a white Christian. Instead, he decries—not the deep faith or the authentic civic belonging of his fellow believers—the terrifying idol of an 'America' that has taken root across the nation. Irwin's Appalachian jeremiad will raise up new leaders for the church and nation."

—Peter Casarella
Professor of Theology, Duke Divinity School

Beyond the Parameters

Beyond the Parameters

Imagining God's World Without America

RICHARD N. IRWIN

WIPF & STOCK · Eugene, Oregon

BEYOND THE PARAMETERS
Imagining God's World Without America

Wipf & Stock
An Imprint of Wipf and Stock Publishers
199 W. 8th Ave., Suite 3
Eugene, OR 97401

www.wipfandstock.com

PAPERBACK ISBN: 979-8-3852-6087-4
HARDCOVER ISBN: 979-8-3852-6088-1
EBOOK ISBN: 979-8-3852-6089-8

VERSION NUMBER 02/17/26

Dedicated to The Ekklesia Project
My friends who ruined my life and gave me hope

Contents

Acknowledgments

Special thanks to Dr. Kelly Waldrop of the Publish House for her invaluable editing and insights. She helped me write what I wanted to write. Thanks to Professor Peter Casarella and Mr. Rodney Clapp, a new friend and an old one who agreed to be my readers. Thanks to Will Willimon and Stanley Hauerwas. *Resident Aliens* redirected my life. Finally, thanks to my family and congregations who have persevered patiently through this project.

Introduction

The book of Jeremiah is a witness to some of the darkest days of the Jews and their promised land. It was some of the darkest days of the promise of sovereignty of God. Will God bless the whole world through, and still include, this people? During Jeremiah's life, what was left of Judah, Jerusalem, and Solomon's Temple were desolated and desecrated. The leadership was taken into exile in Babylon. Jeremiah ended up in Egypt. The holy experiment of God creating a nation of people called to witness to God's will being done on earth as in heaven had all but ended. Jeremiah was told to speak both words of darkness and words of hope in the middle of the despair and destruction. Almost everything will be, and was, lost. Almost.

America and the church that worships within its borders is in a similar historical time. Given the rapid events that have take place since January 20, 2025, this is not a hard argument to make. The following explores portions of the book of Jeremiah and its explanation of what caused the destruction, some of its consequences, and hope for the future, alongside a parallel analysis of the current times and implications for the church in America. God's power and sovereignty are proclaimed along the way. I will attempt to harmonize biblical exegesis, proclamation, and theology. The three foundations will illuminate a truthful analysis of the present and probable future. Leaders will be challenged to lead with hope in a time of profound loss.

Chapter 1 exegetes Jer 10:1–16 concerning idols and the dangers of idolatry. It follows with an essay relating the work of William Cavanaugh and Eugene McCarraher on the subject. The sermon pulls the two sections together and offers a vision of hopeful leadership for the church today.

Chapter 2 exegetes Jer 25:15–29, exploring God's "cup of wrath" poured out on Judah and all the other nations. The essay treats work from Willie James Jennings, Kelly Baker, and Joe Moore and engages the violence caused by the idolatry of racism. The sermon brings the two together with some guidance for current-day leadership.

The between chapters excursus are some mystical experiences. The meaning of them is still being revealed. Their purpose here is to bear witness that the God who called and commanded Jeremiah to speak is still very much alive and well today. The word has not finished its task.

Chapter 3 begins with an exegesis of Jer 51:1–10 and God's judgment on Babylon. The essay draws on the arguments of William Stringfellow and Michael Budde to demonstrate that the American Empire is facing a similar fate. The sermon delves into the depths of a worse-case scenario and proclaims the central importance of faithful leadership.

Chapter 4 is an exegesis of Jer 31:23–40 on the subject of hope. The essay brings into discussion the work of Stanley Hauerwas, Michael Budde, and Will Willimon who dare to speak of a better day coming. The sermon pivots to hope in a renewed relationship with God.

Underneath all of this is the importance of leadership. Jeremiah was a leader even though he was an aberrant one. His leadership was to speak God's word whether anyone followed it or not. He was called to speak words that both tore down and built up. His words came to pass. His words speak truth to our world today.

CHAPTER 1

IDOLATRY

The root cause that led to the threat of annihilation of what is left of Israel, namely Judah and Jerusalem, is an old one: idolatry. Jeremiah often returns to this sin, but a central passage is found in the first sixteen verses of chapter 10. I begin this discussion of idolatry with an exegesis of those sixteen verses. Following that exegesis, I explore idolatry today. Bad or false worship is leading God's people down a similar path—a path that leads to death. But there is hope. The last section is a sermon on Jer 10:1–16 and Jesus' reminder to love God and our neighbor as ourselves.

One of the key challenges in interacting with the book of Jeremiah is revelations about the character of God. Much of my work in this thesis concentrates on the period following a long, patient period of God asking Israel to repent. Much of this work will look at God's acts of destruction. There is, however, mystery to this. At the end of chapter 2, I have included an excursus that witnesses to the relationship between mysticism and violence.

EXEGESIS: JEREMIAH 10:1–16

This exegesis of Jer 10:1–16 will seek to lay a biblical foundation on the topic of idolatry. Idolatry has a long and perilous history that continues through today. In some ways, it is an ancient word representing an ancient world—images made and then worshiped. Walter Brueggemann argues that our current age is not as separate from these times as we might think. The problem in our age is not atheism but idolatry. Underneath the idolatry is self. We want to be God.[1] To deepen the definition of idolatry, William Cavanaugh argues that we all worship, and we all worship badly.[2] The exegesis below roots itself in the ancient world of idolatry, but with some understanding of its relevance to us today. The passage gives a faithful comparison of idols to Israel's God, YHWH. Idols continue to threaten the worship of and service to the One true God today.

Verse 1 of Jer 10 reads, "Hear the word that the LORD speaks to you, O house of Israel." What does it mean to "hear"? What if the speech is so disturbing that it cannot be heard and, therefore, cannot be acted upon in a way that creates a reality not present before the word was spoken? The original audience for this passage is the family of Jacob, the children of Abraham. And the One who speaks to them is the same One who spoke to Moses at the burning bush. It is the same One who delivered them from slavery and made them a people. This God is once again speaking to these people. Verse 2 continues, "Thus says the LORD: Do not learn the way of the nations or be dismayed at the signs of the heavens; for the nations are dismayed at them." It is hard to say if this verse is a warning, judgment, or an encouragement. If Israel is being tempted to follow the nations at the "signs of the heavens,"[3] there is a word from the God from whom they have heard before. Do not follow the ways of those who now seem to have more power than you—or have what you want. In reference to the above questions, there is also revealed an assumption that Israel is capable of not only hearing but learning. From whom shall they learn?

1. Brueggemann, *Jeremiah*, 102.

2. Cavanaugh, *Uses of Idolatry*, loc. 1.

3. "The opening verse it is specifically understood to be the omens and portents that come forth from astronomical phenomena, a major dimension of Babylonian religion as attested by the many astrological and astronomical texts from Mesopotamia." Miller, "Jeremiah," 660.

The term "the way" carries much meaning in both the Old and New Testaments.[4] Here, in Jer 10, there is "the way" of the LORD that Jeremiah is reminding the people of, and there is the way of the other nations. "The Way" is the providential future of creation where God's will is done on earth as it is in heaven. Verse 3 declares that turning these events into some sort of word directing them to some sort of way is false. The audience is encouraged not to be afraid nor listen to the interpretation of these events, as these are lies. They should hear the One who created all that is in the sky.

The second part of verse 3 makes a vast transitional jump: "a tree from the forest is cut down and worked with an ax by the hands of an artisan." Jeremiah and the LORD go from signs in the sky to an ordinary, everyday event. This shift may be to reveal how easy it is to move from celestial movements to someone cutting down a tree and shaping it.[5]

The celestial signs and the wooden figure share this in common: the people are told to "listen to them." Jeremiah looks to undermine this direction by revealing what goes on behind the scenes. This "god" is given "power" (narrated by its creators) to interpret and channel the portents in the sky, starting as a block of wood. It is a false narrative.

Verse 4, according to Brueggemann,[6] brings in economics. Little is said about what sort of shape the wood is formed into. Much is said about what it is covered with. Silver and gold have held exceptional value from before the days of Jeremiah to the present. A beautifully carved wooden figure can be appreciated and even adored. Covered in silver or gold or both, it moves toward celestial events in importance. It now has a universally accepted worth. While this will be discussed in the next section of this chapter, Eugene McCarraher's *The Enchantments of Mammon: How Capitalism Became the Religion of Modernity* argues that

4. Miller, "Jeremiah," 662.

5. Holladay, *Jeremiah 1*, 12.

6. Brueggemann, *Jeremiah*, 103.

silver and gold (and all that come with them) can easily take on a godlike presence.[7]

The text will not allow us to admire these elements for long: "they fasten it [the carved silver and gold covered block of wood] with hammer and nails so that it cannot move" (v. 4). The Revised English Bible says it is fixed this way "to keep them from toppling over."[8] At this point, the text's mocking of the idols is more explicit.[9] Whether this is a warning, a judgment, or an encouragement, the text is trying to create an awareness in the listeners of reality. This is a carefully crafted piece of an ordinary tree that has value because of the silver and gold—value that could have been directed elsewhere.

The mockery continues in verse 5: "Their idols are like scarecrows in a cucumber field, and they cannot speak; they have to be carried for they cannot walk." According to Holladay, the text has moved from awesome signs in the sky to an idol to a scarecrow.[10] Its authority to guide human and national direction has been revealed as a lie.

It would be a mistake to undervalue these phenomena and creations, however. Who has not been overwhelmed by the night sky or the sight of a storm? Who has not been moved by the beauty of a work of art or a worship room, especially one that includes precious metals or jewels? Even the lowly scarecrow has value. A cucumber diet would not be celebrated, but it is better than trying to eat wood or gold. It is when a people or a nation become delusional and believe that which is not God *is* God that a word needs to be spoken.

As the text reveals these idols, we are told once again, in verse 5b, not to be afraid of them: "for they cannot do evil, nor is it in them to do good." These creations cannot act in any way. There is no need to fear, much less adore, something that is incapable of creating, giving direction, or forming a people.

7. McCarraher, *Enchantments of Mammon*, 3.

8. Jer 10:4, REB.

9. Holladay, *Jeremiah 1*, 100.

10. Holladay, *Jeremiah 1*, 12.

There is another sudden shift at verse 6: "There is none like you, O LORD; you are great, and your name is great in might." We have a description of the idols, and then we have YHWH—the God of Abraham, Isaac, and Jacob; the God of David and Jeremiah; the God some of us name Trinity. Unlike the idols, which vary from beautiful works of art laden with economic value to scarecrows in cucumber patches, we hear the declarative: There is none like You! Unlike the idols, in which the nations of this world put their faith and by which Israel is either tempted or in which it has already put its faith, the one true God is unique. The difference is that YHWH is alive. The great name of the LORD is called out in a unique way than the way of idols. Verse 7 adds a piece of the job description of God: King of nations. This political statement moves beyond Israel to include the nations whose gods Israel is being warned about. There is a claim that YHWH is not only Israel's God but is God of those who have taken or will take Israel into exile. This God can act. The others cannot.

Brueggemann notes that

> characteristically, the Bible does not deny the existence of other gods. The Bible assumes that the world is polytheistic. The other gods exist. They have seductive power, but what they lack is power for life. They cannot do anything, and in that decisive test they are utterly unlike Yahweh, who has the power to give life and there also the power to judge life.[11]

Returning to verse 7, it says, "Who would not fear you, O King of the nations?" The English word "fear" brings up several theological avenues. English nuances include "awe" or "revere." Perhaps much depends on where one stands in relationship to God. Occasionally, I will hear and then see a military helicopter flying by. That machine is awesome and capable of firing weapons. It would invoke a much different "fear" flying into space where those weapons will be discharged. Similarly, in this passage, immense power is ascribed to the LORD who will discharge that

11. Brueggemann, *Jeremiah*, 102–3.

power as desired. Unlike the helicopter, the LORD's use of power is much more mysterious. God's power and timing rarely coincide with ours. It could be argued that part of the turn toward idols may be linked to YHWH's inconsistency in behaving according to human directions and schedule. Verses 6 and 7 introduce the God capable of both protection and destruction—a God who acts in comparison to a god who may look beautiful, intimidating, awe inspiring but is unable to speak or act. "For that is Your due," concludes verse 7b. This God is due respect, awe, and some sort of fear.

The second part of verse 7 links the leadership with YHWH. There are wise ones among the nations (whether these are general leaders, kings, or even the skilled artisans who create idols is not clear) who have created or inherited kingdoms. None of them can compare with YHWH. In Jeremiah's day, a shift was happening between Assyria and Babylon. Egypt was also in the mix. These real nations possessed large armies and had powerful economic systems. The people of Jeremiah's time had watched their rise and fall, and their gods along with them. Jeremiah's audience is warned and encouraged at the same time. The warning is not to place faith in the physical and emotional power of Babylon and Egypt. The encouragement is that this power is temporary. It is only for a season.

Verse 8 bounces back into the critique of the idols, along with humans who may include artisans, leaders, and even kings: they are all stupid and foolish. This implies ignorance alongside immorality. The most dangerous people are those who think they know what they are doing but don't.[12] Part of the stupidity and foolishness is using labor and resources for something that is not only useless but also contains an immense potential for harm. It is stupid and foolish to lead people to put their faith in something that is not capable of helping or guiding them.

This issue presents a complex problem. When a people offer sacrifices to a god for rain and it rains, does this not prove the god's power? Likewise, when sacrifices are offered to YHWH for the

12. I must credit a deceased church member from Piney Woods, North Carolina, Rayford Isenhower, for this expression. God rest his soul.

same request and a drought continues, does this not create enough doubt to look to other gods for help? Jeremiah goes to the root issue, which is leadership. The gods are empowered (even though it is the power of death) by the artisan creating them and, we may assume, other leaders, including the king, worshiping them and leading others to do the same. As part of his leadership, Jeremiah reminds the reader that it is a block of wood. All people who worship anything other than the LORD are both stupid and immoral or become that way by bringing these idols into existence.

Verse 9 goes back into detail about idol manufacturing. "Beaten silver is brought from Tarshish and gold from Uphaz." One of these towns is known, the other not.[13] That these elements are mentioned a second time in this short passage may underline Brueggemann's thesis that idolatry warps God's economics. Gold and silver were used to encourage the worship of blocks of wood, to turn the hearts, minds, and bodies away from the care of widows and orphans. It is not a move toward those having much not having too much and those having little not having too little.[14]

The second half of verse 9, "their clothing is blue and purple," links these idols directly to royalty.[15] Jeremiah is returning to a theme that idol worship involves: "But the Lord is the true God: he is the living God and the everlasting King" (v. 10). Here we have a true God, not a false one, an alive God, not a dead block of wood, no matter how well adorned. Finally, the verse makes a political claim: YHWH is the everlasting King, not these temporary ones that may or may not lead the people faithfully. The second half of verse 9 returns to the theme of fear: "At his wrath the earthquakes and the nations cannot endure his indignation." This is a King who not only cares but a King who can scare the nations of this world. It is a King who can and does destroy nations (as verse 10 proclaims).

While it is beyond the parameters of this book, giving God the credit for "natural" scary events also opens God up for the blame. Can it be that God is in the hurricane *and* in the cleanup

13. Fretheim, *Jeremiah*, 170.

14. 2 Cor 8:15.

15. Lundbom, *Jeremiah 1–20*, 586.

help? Jeremiah is clear that it is a God who acts in ways that creates fear in peoples and our leaders, but also a God to be listened to.

Verse 11 is unique in that it is the only Aramaic verse in the book of Jeremiah.[16] Commentators do not agree on its original audience or purpose. It reads, "The gods who did not make the heavens and the earth shall perish from the earth and from under the heavens." If directed at Israel, this is a warning to either not worship the gods of the nations, especially Babylon, Egypt, and Assyria, or to repent from doing so. If it is directed toward the nations for whom Israel has been exiled, it is a liturgy of protection for exiled Israel—words to be spoken in Aramaic so that other nations can hear and understand.[17] I suggest this important verse may be used in many ways at contrasting times. It may serve as a warning to both Israel and the other nations. It sums up the first ten verses and provides a bridge to the next passage. It also carries eschatological judgment. Idols are ending.

Verse 12 circles back to YHWH: "It is he who made the earth by his power who established the world by his wisdom and by his understanding stretched out the heavens." The LORD makes the earth, not idols. The LORD has power, not silent blocks of wood that need to be carried about. The LORD has wisdom. The idols and their cohort are stupid and foolish. The LORD stretches out the heavens. The nations are teaching others to be afraid of how the heavens are arranged. Jeremiah is saying be afraid of the One who made them.

Verse 13 describes a God who simply speaks for action to happen—action that no person, not even a king, can perform. Rain, mist, and lightning all respond to YHWH's words. This is an awe-inspiring word as well as a hopeful one. Later in the book, Jeremiah will be more explicit about hope.

Verse 14 declares, "Everyone is stupid and without knowledge; goldsmiths are all put to shame by their idols; for their images are false, and there is no breath in them." To use a contemporary example, evidence is coming in about the tactics of those who are

16. Lundbom, *Jeremiah 1–20*, 593.

17. Fretheim, *Jeremiah*, 170.

accelerating climate collapse. Their greed and claims to power are both stupid and foolish. Once again, raising the tricky question of God commanding the elements of this world, what if tornados, hurricanes, and other disasters are a warning for the nations to head in a different direction? At what point will the people throw the idols and their makers away? When will we see that these are false and there is no breath in them?

Jeremiah, in verse 15, is not vague about the outcome of these false gods, along with their promises and makers: "They are worthless, a work of delusion; at the time of their punishment, they shall perish." This is a word of both warning and hope. The days of the false promises made by idols and those who lead us toward placing our hope in them are numbered.

The back and forth ends in verse 16 with one more description of the LORD as "the portion of Jacob." Most of the commentators connect this claim to an intimate relationship with Israel, even using the pre-wrestling match name.[18] This God has an intimate relationship with this people. And when they are faithful, they are intimate with God as well. Perhaps even with each other. Whether or not Israel has fallen into idolatry at this point, we know eventually they do. This intimate claim, naming God as "the portion of Jacob," has profound depth at any point along that path. R. E. Clements describes it best:

> Both in its essential character and in its practical implications idolatry becomes inseparably linked with a departure from the grounds for Israel's existence as a people. It is no longer simply a practical turning aside to a different tradition of religion but a deeper spiritual and intellectual denial of the nature of reality.[19]

Idolatry and delusion coincide. This is especially true when that which is not God is claimed to be God.

As I will argue in the next section, idolatry is not limited to the pre-exilic and exilic peoples of the sixth century BCE. I work

18. Gen 32:25–33.

19. Clements, *Jeremiah*, 68.

in a place and time where God's name is used all over—from sea to shining sea. When asked, most in our community would identify as Christians. Most would also deny that violence, nationalism, capitalism, and a host of other "isms" compete for devotion to the Trinity. We will look at the truthfulness of that denial next.

CAPITALISM AS IDOLATRY

Jeremiah's concern about idolatry may seem antiquated to us. Two thousand five hundred years ago, well before the Enlightenment, people made beautiful, even monetarily valuable, statues and worshiped them as gods. We know better today. William Cavanaugh argues otherwise in his 2024 book *The Uses of Idolatry*. Idolatry is practiced today, and we may see similar destructive outcomes later witnessed in Jeremiah. The most dangerous idol of our day is capitalism. It is a threat to our relationship with God. It is a threat to our relationship with our neighbors. It is a threat to our relationship with creation. It is a threat to our relationship with ourselves. It is a carefully crafted, often beautiful idol we worship so devoutly that it is hard to recognize our adoration. It is the water in which we swim. Eugene McCarraher has offered significant help in uncovering this reality. In his 2019 book *The Enchantments of Mammon: How Capitalism Became the Religion of Modernity*, McCarraher traces capitalism through the Enlightenment and clearly shows its "religious" character. In this essay, I explore these works and how the distance between us and the idols Jeremiah wrote about is not as far as we think—or have been led to believe.

Awareness could lead to repentance. Jesus can help us. In all three synoptic Gospels, he is asked to identify the greatest commandment: "You shall love the Lord your God with all your heart, and with all your soul, and with all your mind. And the second is like it: You shall love your neighbor as yourself" (Matt 22:34–40; Mark 12:28–31; Luke 10:27). All three Gospels are a witness of Jesus living out those commandments surrounded by failed attempts of others to do the same. Idolatry misdirects love.

In our defense, loving an invisible God is a big ask. We have stories from Scripture. Many have had personal conversion experiences when God chooses to reveal Godself in a way that makes resisting God almost impossible. Christians could argue that, in Jesus of Nazareth, God has been made very visible. However, we have a long testimony of the challenge. Where is God visible right now? How can we love a God with everything we have and are when Jesus is in heaven along with all the great cloud of witnesses who have demonstrated this love and devotion, even to the point of death?

Cavanaugh is sympathetic to our situation. Citing the essay "True Faith in God," Cavanaugh writes, "Following an invisible God is hard; it exhausts the human capacity to be patient and to live with uncertainty and a lack of signs that appeal to our material nature."[20] We are asked to follow with every breath we take a God whose presence must often be revealed by faith. Combine that with some history of God using God's freedom *not* to be present (Jesus calling out the temporary abandonment from the cross, among other stories), and it takes an extremely mature faith to love this God with every breath we take. Everything. Even if we risk abandonment in the end.

Is it any wonder we turn to idols? Jeremiah's world had them. However, he and God argue in chapter 10 that they are useless. To jump forward about 2,500 years, McCarraher will not blame modern belief in capitalism as a religion completely on the Protestant reformation, but he comes close. Specifically, he focuses on the Puritans as the seeds.[21] Under the motivation of "improvement" and "progress," the Puritans eventually began substituting the accumulation of wealth, along with all the physical objects that came with it (especially land), for the invisible God. Added to that desire was an interpretation of Calvinism that all of this was predestined as God's will takes us down the road where Jeremiah has already arrived: a beautiful gold and silver-covered god who cannot speak, move, or save. But it is a god who can be seen. We claim this god

20. Cavanaugh, *Uses of Idolatry*, loc. 140.

21. McCarraher, *Enchantments of Mammon*, 31.

has made life "better." We have learned to love that god with all our hearts, with all our minds, and with all our souls.

Cavanaugh is less sympathetic to our plight in the chapter analyzing Augustine's teaching on idolatry:

> The human making of gods is an attempt to bring God down to a human level while elevating humans to a god-like level; we want to have gods that serve human desires rather than the other way around. Pride and idolatry are therefore intertwined.[22]

Mentioned here and elsewhere, Gen 3:5 is a scriptural launching point for this condition. Humanity's desire to be more than we are combines with a crafty lie from the serpent that we will be God if we eat of the tree in the middle of the garden. The birth of sin in the world is our attempt at self-deification.[23]

Capitalism is a voracious feeding trough for self-indulgence and a vain attempt at self-deification. If it has a nature, it is that enough is never enough. There must always be "growth." There must always be one more thing just out of our grasp that will finally let us be God. That quest has led us to the brink of making God's creation uninhabitable to humans.

McCarraher's work reveals an additional blindness to this when Christianity is used to cover up this idol. While his book is filled with hundreds of examples, one of the most outstanding is the witness of John D. Rockefeller, founder of Standard Oil, today known as Exxon and BP. Giving a brief analysis of his family of origin, McCarraher, quotes the richest person in the world during his time in response to the money "God gave him": "The whole process seems a miracle! What a blessing oil has been to mankind!"[24] As I write this a century later, idolatry has led us down a tragic path. This is particularly true of leaders like Rockefeller. McCarraher

22. Cavanaugh, *Uses of Idolatry*, loc. 158.

23. Cavanaugh, *Uses of Idolatry*, loc. 176.

24. McCarraher, *Enchantments of Mammon*, 194.

sums up his mention of Rockefeller as "another synthesis of Protestant enchantment and pecuniary reason.[25]

McCarraher's whole book could be summed up as a failed attempt to serve both God and *mammon*. (See Matt 6:24 and Luke 16:13 for Jesus' teaching on the subject.) More to the point, we see throughout a failure to love God with everything we are and have. That love has shifted to something that is not God.

THE BINDING OF CAPITALISM AND NATIONALISM

The idolatry of capitalism also leads to a failure to love our neighbor. Our best failed attempt to love our neighbor may be found in the idolatry of nationalism. Cavanaugh calls this a "splendid" idolatry, as it is devotion to something outside of ourselves.[26] The complexities of Cavanaugh's work are evident throughout but especially in this chapter. Nationalism points individuals away from selfishness and self-centeredness while at the same time leading us toward "lethal levels of devotion toward what is not God."[27]

As a Southerner, it is hard to imagine life without nationalism. I grew up surrounded by the flag and spent much of my youth pledging allegiance to it. I never gave it much thought until I began to listen to Stanley Hauerwas.[28] The flag can be seductive. It can energize the desire to see America as more than it is. It also gives us an avenue to love both neighbor and stranger. We are Americans, and that identity assumes a mutual devotion to the nation. An equally powerful devotion includes love for our region of the country. "American by birth, Southern by the Grace of God!" was a popular sentiment growing up and can still be found today, manifest with the display and devotion to another more controversial flag.

25. McCarraher, *Enchantments of Mammon*, 195.

26. Cavanaugh, *Uses of Idolatry*, loc. 218.

27. Cavanaugh, *Uses of Idolatry*, loc. 218.

28. See Hauerwas, *War and the American Difference*, and many other of his writings.

Cavanaugh traces the movement of devotion from the church to the nation. As the United Methodist Church has continued to shrink and recently divide, we can easily see the migration. Part of the attraction is rooted in virtue. It is identified as "splendid" because of the call to "fidelity to something larger than oneself, devotion to one's fellow citizens, and a willingness to sacrifice oneself for others."[29] It is a kind of love of neighbor that is not rooted and sustained in the unconditional love of God.

The consequences of that lack of rootedness leaves the neighbor and the nation vulnerable to a different kind of idolatry. While it is in transition, the last forty years of capitalism have been described as "neoliberal," a period known for "trickle-down economics" or "unfettered markets." McCarraher gives a very thorough history of its invention and growth.

One of the early leaders he describes is Ayn Rand. Influenced by Nietzsche and his philosophy of power, Rand joined a chorus of reaction against the New Deal. While her work deserves more time, for my purposes, I see her as a bridge between one idol and another. In her work, the God/*mammon* partnership is abandoned. The individual is praised as the source of creativity, action, and accumulation. Rand understood that something needed to take the place of God. "In her way, Rand was a theologian, bringing to a graceless apogee the American divinization of power that began with Emerson."[30] In this view, the neighbor is a pragmatic being that may or may not be helpful in my self-fulfillment. At worse, the neighbor is a competitor. It will be up to me to decide that. Love has been abandoned. Part of Rand's extremism and urgency is rooted in her experience of totalitarianism in the Soviet Union.

While ironically not alone, Rand's influence carries into the public forum today. I could point the reader toward either *The Fountainhead* novel or movie, but another place her voice speaks into popular culture is through the work of the rock band Rush and its lyricist Neil Peart. Their multi-platinum 1976 album *2112* was dedicated to Rand. A story of a future dystopian society where

29. Cavanaugh, *Uses of Idolatry*, loc. 218.

30. McCarraher, *Enchantments of Mammon*, 602.

religion and government create an impenetrable team, controlling society, a lone soul discovers a guitar in a cave. The creativity of music brings color into a grey world. Describing a narrative of the lone individual who bravely stands against the authorities was a common theme in Peart's writing. His work influenced a generation of disaffected people who rebelled against the blandness, if not oppression of the authorities. The surviving members of the group have blown up the internet by offering a tour in 2026 that will keep this view before millions.

Peart's voice was one of many. George Orwell's *1984*, trusted folk leader Paul Harvey's coining the phrase "Reaganomics," and many others gave leadership to the myth of the individual taking a stand against the "institution," "the man," "the government," etc., which helps explain the loss of love of neighbor. In an attempt at rebelling against repressive control, individualism threatens to take its place.

Referring back to Rand, this did not happen by accident:

> "A new faith is needed," as she confided in her journals, "a definite, positive set of new values and a new interpretation of life." "We will give people a faith," she once wrote to a friend, "a positive, clear, and consistent system of belief." . . . Rand was indeed a pioneer in her nomination of the dollar as a worthy and durable surrogate.[31]

Jeremiah saw more than one artisan who created more than one idol. Rand is in that contemporary company. In her world, God is dead, and the neighbor is rarely known and certainly not trusted, much less loved. As for love, two (love of God and love of neighbor) of our three pathways to Trinity have been traded in for idols. We now turn to the love of self.

Much of the above discussion may be rooted in the idolatry of self. Cavanaugh sums up Augustine's understanding: "For Augustine, idolatry—despite its outward appearance as dedication to something other than the self—is rooted in a kind of self-love,

31. McCarraher, *Enchantments of Mammon*, 602.

though one that paradoxically results in the dissolution of self."[32] This view fits well into McCarraher's story of capitalism. The worship of this idol finally leads us to the mirror. Identity as a beloved child of God and a sibling to neighbor has been traded for the individual consumer. Our worth is now found in our ability to earn and spend money. The dangers of this are frightening. Cavanaugh begins his work with a quote from David Foster Wallace's 2005 commencement address at Kenyon College:

> In the day-to-day trenches of adult life, there is no such thing as atheism. There is no such thing as not worshipping. Everybody worships. The only choice we get is what to worship. And the compelling reason for choosing some sort of god or spiritual-type thing to worship . . . is that pretty much anything else you worship will eat you alive.[33]

Being eaten alive seems to be an accurate description of the times in which we find ourselves. The idol of community was torn down and replaced by the idol of individualism, which is the heartbeat of American nationalism and the sustainer of capitalism. Neoliberal economics was branded as "freedom to choose" with no restricted regulations. It has led to the largest wealth gap in recent history.[34] The climate is collapsing.[35] The goal of capitalism is unlimited growth. We have created and unleashed an insatiable beast with its eye on the next quarter's profit. The meaning it provides is a far cry from loving God and neighbor.

However, it is difficult to blame the individual for this. We will look at the principalities and powers later, but for now, I will ask, is it possible to love oneself without idolatry? For Augustine

32. Cavanaugh, *Uses of Idolatry*, loc. 158.

33. Cavanaugh, *Uses of Idolatry*, loc. 1.

34. Lu, "Visualizing Wealth Distribution"; Kent, "State of U.S. Household Wealth."

35. This was the focus of 2024's Ekklesia Project gathering entitled "Bearing Witness to Grief: Climate Collapse, Resistance, and Grounded Hope." The United Nations website presents a variety of reports on climate collapse: United Nations, "Climate Reports."

and many other theologians and spiritual leaders, the answer may be no. We can only find our life by losing it (Matt 10:39). On top of that we have the example of Jesus giving up his life for all. It would be a stretch to say that Jesus hated himself, however. How can the second person of the Trinity possess anything but love, including for himself?

Cavanaugh may point us in a helpful direction: "Idolatry is usually a matter of degree . . . [an] inordinate devotion to some created thing instead of the Creator."[36] What has been marketed as self-love and self-fulfillment reveals itself as an idol. Linked with the desire for things, self-love becomes an end. It is eating us and our world alive.

I will explore a pathway out of this dilemma in chapter four. For now, I take a deeper look at how idolatry leads toward a false love of self. This false love treads into the saving acts of Jesus with atonement theology. While it is beyond this essay to discuss that doctrine in detail, its practical application in the Southern Appalachian Methodist church has led to a kind of cheap grace that can turn the self into a kind of "saving" god.

Intricately connected to this is the idol of "freedom." That word cojoins nationalism to capitalism. Freedom is not an idol in itself. It is a matter of degree. Freedom is a gift from God until it becomes an end. Where the line is crossed is blurry. I write this a few days after July 4, 2024. One of the most popular Christian congregations in our area hosted a "Freedom Fest" that gave a witness to the combination of nationalism, individualism, and a part of Christianity that emphasizes the atoning blood of Jesus above all other doctrines.

Two symbols are vital in this witness. The flag (and all its derivatives) of the United States of America stands for "freedom," but as written above, in this iteration, it is the freedom of the individual to do or be or act in whatever way one chooses. The invisible force of capitalism influences and can coerce that choice. The cross, in this witness, stands for freedom for that choice to

36. Cavanaugh, *Uses of Idolatry*, loc. 307.

continue eternally. The flag tells me I am free in this life. The cross tells me I get to continue doing whatever I want forever.

Genesis 3:4 has come full circle. Or it never left. When the self becomes an idol, we have traded the gifted love from the eternal God for a love that consumes itself. It may be beautiful or not, but eventually, it is found to be just a scarecrow guarding the cucumber patch (Jer 10:5). Trying to find love of oneself in things leads to the type of "unsplendid" idolatry Cavanaugh discusses.[37]

Consumerism as idolatry is different from biblical idolatry because, instead of attachment to the false god, it is attachment/detachment from things. Or put more accurately, it is temporarily attaching to things, detaching, then attaching to a new thing. Consumerism is a large idol that creates infinite smaller idols.[38] Taking the place of Rockefeller, Jeff Bezos's Amazon provides this service to us today. Naming the warehouses from which these idols magically appear on our doorstep "fulfillment centers"[39] gives us some idea of the hopes of this sort of idolatrous self-love. But fulfillment never comes. If we are ever satisfied for long, the idol topples over.

In his epilogue, McCarraher describes the global idol that the "freedom" of the individual idol has helped create:

> The American Century morphed into the neoliberal Market Everlasting: unfettered free trade and globalization . . . the privatization of public services and their lucrative relegation to the caprice of the marketplace; the "reinvention" of government agencies along the lines of corporate bureaucracies; and the maniacal deregulation of finance and industry under the rubric of "modernization," liberating corporations from "stifling" restrictions on their freedom to invest, pollute, and exploit.[40]

We are being eaten alive with our own individual selves as one of the courses.

37. Cavanaugh, *Uses of Idolatry*, loc. 280–331.
38. Cavanaugh, *Uses of Idolatry*, loc. 280.
39. Cavanaugh, *Uses of Idolatry*, loc. 15.
40. McCarraher, *Enchantments of Mammon*, 663.

In this essay, I have engaged two contemporary scholars, one theologian and one historian, to show the relevance of Jeremiah's warning to Judah some 2,600 years ago. There were overwhelming, desperate consequences in Jeremiah's time, and we can see similar ones today. Those will be explored in the next two chapters. This chapter concludes with a sermon that brings the gospel into the conversation. Just as Jeremiah was told to offer the people a choice, so we have one today. Will we continue the worship of idols, or shall we repent and worship the one true God? The hour is late, but there is another path.

LOVING GOD AND NEIGHBOR OR LOVING IDOLS? A SERMON ON JEREMIAH 10:1–16 AND MATTHEW 22:37–39

Jeremiah had a tough preaching job. His call to be a leader was even harder. God's people had wandered away from the witness they were called to be. They were supposed to be a living example of God's will being done on earth as in heaven. In Jeremiah's time, they were failing. They were lost.

In chapter 10, Jeremiah, acting as a spokesperson for God, lays the blame on idolatry. Israel (more specifically, Judah, in this case, as Israel had already dissolved) had stopped loving God with all their hearts, with all their minds, with all their souls. They had mixed allegiances at best. They had abandoned the LORD at worst. They had become like other nations or were about to.

Jeremiah begins with a warning from the LORD in verses 2 and 3: "Do not learn the way of the nations or be dismayed at the signs of the heavens. For the customs of the people are false. A tree is cut down and shaped by a skilled artist then covered in silver and gold."

When I think of worshiping idols, I think, well, that was a long time ago when people did not know any better. We know better today. In his 2024 book *The Uses of Idolatry*, William Cavanaugh, one of the leading theologians in the church today, says otherwise.

Cavanaugh argues that our lives and world are filled with potential idols that can and do mislead us from the one true God.

The problem, he argues, is a matter of degree. We would laugh today if we put a statue, no matter how beautiful, in this sanctuary and said, this is God: bow down to this statue. However, how would you feel if we moved the flag of the United States out of the sanctuary or at least out of the area with our other worship symbols? I can tell you I have tried that before! There was rage and a veiled threat to replace me as pastor. I have not mentioned it again until today.

The degree of idolatry involved depends on where love or appreciation for anything, including America, crosses over into a kind of worship—a move from our Creator being worshiped to something that was created being worshiped—in this case a nation and its symbol, the flag.

Jesus may help us with this. He was asked by the leadership in his day about what is most important. They too lived in a time when their nation's existence was under threat. For them, the object of adoration was not a flag but the temple. The love of the temple and all it symbolized was at least in competition for devotion with the One they worshiped there.

Jesus lays it out straight for them and for us: the most important thing is to love God with everything we have and love our neighbor as ourselves. When we start there and finish there, our relationship with everything else changes. Going back to the flag, we can move toward gratitude for the land of our birth and away from putting it above our relationship with God and neighbor.

Jeremiah encourages all of us to make that move in verses 6 and 7: "There is none like you, O LORD; you are great, and your name is great in might. Who would not fear you, O King of the nations? For that is your due; among all the wise ones of the nations and in all their kingdoms, there is no one like you."

There is no nation, or symbol, or people that can compete with God, but that does not stop us from trying! One of the freedoms we celebrate when we consider the flag is our way of life. For most of us hearing this message, it is an incredibly good life—a wonderfully comfortable life. As I write this sermon, I sit in a comfortable recliner inside a lovely, air-conditioned parsonage. If anything, I have too much to eat. Most importantly, I am safe. Probably more so than I am aware, the flag and what it stands for helps all of that happen for me, for my family, and for my neighbor. Most, if not all of us, can say the same.

Likewise, the flag stands for an economic system that allows me to "fill in the gaps" with a quick trip to Walmart or a few minutes with Amazon. It places me in a dilemma of being both a creature whose Creator desires for me to enjoy this "modern" life and a consumer whose voraciousness threatens to destroy creation for all. Enough is never enough.

Eugene McCarraher, a history professor at Villanova University, has written a history of capitalism entitled *The Enchantments of Mammon: How Capitalism Became the Religion of Modernity.* He tells a bit of the story of John D. Rockefeller. In his day, Rockefeller became the richest person in the world. And he was a devout Christian. In his life, we can see this struggle between loving God and neighbor competing with making as much money as possible. Rockefeller tried to do both. Historians lean toward him being much more successful at the latter.

Jesus warns us about trying to serve God and *mammon* in Matt 6:24. He says it is impossible. Rockefeller and other leaders, and perhaps we as well, have tried the truth of Jesus' warning. I believe we have crossed the line in our world today. We say one thing yet act in a way that is contradictory. We have traded an active love of God and love of neighbor for a love of a nation and its economics that provide us with a lot of stuff and the safety to enjoy it—if we can ever get enough.

Jeremiah warns us in the second half of verse 14 that our stuff has no breath. It cannot save us. A flag cannot save us. A nation cannot save us. An economic system cannot save us. Only the one true God can save us.

Jesus gets us pointed back in the right direction when he reminds us to love God with all that we have and love our neighbor as ourselves. We can use this teaching to question our behavior and, with some help, change it.[41]

Jeremiah tells us these idols, these things are "a work of delusion" (verse 15a). Do you know what a delusion is? That is something we believe is real and is not. Cavanaugh argues that idolatry is alive and well today. McCarraher argues that our stuff and the system that provides our stuff has taken the place of God in our lives or at least threatens to. The dangerous part is that we may not be able to see either, much less act on it.

So here is the good news! Jesus sets the foundation and direction: love God; love your neighbor as yourself. We may have some repenting ahead of us! And the Holy Spirit will help us by reminding us of what we already know and teaching us what we are now ready to learn (John 14:26).

We can begin with a daily recommitment to God. "Please give me knowledge of your will for me, and the power to carry it out" is a useful prayer. If we pray that and trust God will answer it, we may start to see these idols revealed. But more importantly, we open our hearts to the wonder of the one true living God who gave and gives us life, who gives life to others, who gives life to the nations, who gives us the ability to create things to help us enjoy this life.

A second thing we can do is tithe. As United Methodists, we have strayed far from the ancient practice of giving ten percent of our income away. This may be the hardest but most practical push-back to a principality and power that is never satisfied. We live

41. Years ago, when I lived in Durham, a scary and tragic event happened. A homeowner opened a door to the garage and found four youths had broken in and were trying to take things. Golf clubs were mentioned in the news article. He had a rifle handy and opened fire, shooting three of them in the back as they fled, killing two. That the robbers were black and the white homeowner was not charged because of a small child in the house further complicates this story. But my point is, if I am willing to kill *anyone* over a set of golf clubs, I have found an idol. That idol is tempting me to commit murder. Sadly, when I told this story to a congregation a few years back, one of them came up to me afterward to push back—someone who had been in the pews since a child. A follower of Jesus (and a fellow golfer) said to me, "But man, those are your sticks!"

in a system that must always consume, throw away, and consume more. Our founder, John Wesley, started his career making sixteen English pounds a year. He lived off fourteen and gave two away. Later, he was making one hundred pounds a year. He still lived off fourteen and gave the rest away. The average United Methodist, those who claim Wesley as our founder, gives away an average of 2 to 3 percent of their income. Our beliefs and actions do not match.

But Jesus can help us here, too. When we love our neighbor, we are generous. We are generous with our time *and* our money. We have several ministries that we can support more fully, from the parish fund to Yokefellow to UMCOR. If we want to work on a larger scale for public policy changes, we have the Poor People's Campaign, among others—organizations that go beyond charity to address the roots of poverty. There are plenty of opportunities to practice love of neighbor and experience the joy of that for ourselves.

Finally, Jeremiah promises that idols will come and go. They do not last. None of them are like God. His people refused to learn this lesson, and we will look at the consequences of that in a later sermon. For today, we have a choice to make. We have a God who wants to help us. Amen.

CONCLUSION

This chapter explored the problem faced by Jeremiah and us. While it is a brief discussion, I pray the reader will engage with both Cavanaugh and McCarraher if there is any doubt about the practice of idolatry and its most dangerous manifestation, capitalism. In chapter 4, I will open a clearer path of hope. For now, we will need to see one of the consequences of idolatry: violence. Chapter 2 will discuss how the creation of race moves from the worship of deadly gods to violence.

CHAPTER 2

VIOLENCE

Idolatry has consequences. When the people worship a false god, we live inside a lie. Even worse, when we worship a false image of the one true God, we are lost. Below is a discussion of what happens when people are lost. YHWH remains sovereign and will act as sovereign, but it is nearly impossible to form a people who do not recognize that authority, or worse, mistake it for something else.

The arrival of modern racism led directly to the violence necessary to try and repress peoples whose labor and land were stolen. That the God we have revealed in Scripture was brought in to justify all of that is almost beyond belief, yet that is exactly what happened. And there is plenty of evidence it carries on today in a usually, but certainly not always, more subtle way. The sermon is an attempt to recognize that sometimes God's sovereignty includes violence either directly from God or directed by God. However, this is the exception rather than the rule, and for Christians to justify killing means we have stopped following Jesus. The excursus following the sermon is part of my testimony. I believe it reveals a couple of things. First, that Jesus of Nazareth is still alive. Second, that America may one day reap what it has sown. And third, the new creation is coming. It is a testimony of hope before chapter 3.

EXEGESIS OF JEREMIAH 25:15–29

The exegesis of Jer 25:15–29 will give a small interaction on violence. I make no claims to explore that topic thoroughly but acknowledge its reality in Scripture as a basis for partially explaining its existence today. It will also explore the claim that YHWH is sovereign over all nations, not just Israel/Judah. I consider God's complicity in violence, at least to an end as an end, as YHWH claims to be Lord over all peoples, leaders, and nations.

Verse 15 reads, "For thus said the LORD, the God of Israel, to me: 'Take from my hand this cup of the wine of wrath and make all the nations to whom I send you drink it.'" At the beginning, this chapter has theological questions regarding violence. It is a cup of wine and wrath—an angry, violent drink. Holladay notes that the "cup of wrath" and the "cup of wine" are closely related in structure in Hebrew.[1] As we will see below, the violence this cup produces will be much like the violence of someone drunk—staggering, unable to think clearly, beyond rational thought. Patrick Miller comments on the cup of wrath imagery related to how drunkenness "conveys the chaos, loss of control, disintegrations and powerlessness" resulting from this judgment.[2] In this case, the drunkenness affects entire nations. All of the nations.

From the opening line of "thus said," YHWH, the God of Israel, makes the first move. While Israel/Judah's cause for destruction is covered in the previous chapters of Jeremiah (idolatry being among those causes is explored in chapter 1 of this work), the reason behind the judgment of the nations is not given in detail. The nations will receive judgment through a means they understand: violence.

While the LORD initiates the action, Jeremiah is called to participate, as he is ordered to "take from my hand."[3] This is part of Jeremiah's calling to be a prophet to all nations.[4] It is a part of his

1. Holladay, *Jeremiah 1*, 670.
2. Miller, "Jeremiah," 766.
3. Jer 25:15b.
4. Jer 1:5c.

calling to "pluck up and pull down, to destroy and overthrow."[5] It is the will of the LORD for Jeremiah to do more than preach or give a warning. In the taking of the cup of wrath/wine, Jeremiah is called to participate in the judgement and the violence that comes with it. While he will not lift a sword, he stands with the cause for the swords to be used. Jeremiah is to "make all the nations to whom I send you drink it."[6] Below we will see that this mandate to take up the cup will include all nations in the world.

Verse 16 continues, "They shall drink and stagger and go out of their minds because of the sword that I am sending among them." "They" includes all peoples of all nations, but many leaders of specific nations are later specifically mentioned. Leadership matters. As the leaders are made to drink and show the effects of intoxication, the people soon follow. As with the interchangeability of wrath and wine, so it is with drunkenness and the sword. The sword may be a symbol for drunkenness. Berrigan states that the cup and sword are one.[7] Lundbom suggests the drunkenness will leave the nations helpless before the sword that does the finishing work.[8]

In verse 17, Jeremiah comments, "So, I took the cup from the LORD's hand and made all the nations to whom the LORD sent me drink it." Jeremiah is complicit. Fretheim calls this a symbolic action or vision.[9] My concern is Jeremiah's role in this. Does the LORD overwhelm Jeremiah's free will, or is Jeremiah choosing to cooperate? It is here that we begin to encounter the pathos of Jeremiah. Most of Jeremiah's leadership is focused on pronouncing suffering and destruction. At various places in this book, he complains about his calling. In verse 17, he accepts the cup and does what he is told. His feelings are not revealed. However, as Fretheim notes, there is a cooperation of divine and human actions. The destruction will occur at the hands of Nebuchadnezzar

5. Jer 1:10b.

6. Jer 25:15c.

7. Berrigan, *Jeremiah*, 11.

8. Lundbom, *Jeremiah 21–36*, 259.

9. Fretheim, *Jeremiah*, 357.

and Babylon, but it is rooted in the permission of the LORD and Jeremiah speaking that permission into reality.[10]

Verses 18 through 26 list the nations, beginning in verse 18 with God's own chosen people and its capital city: "Jerusalem and the towns of Judah, its kings and officials, to make them a desolation and a waste, an object of hissing and of cursing, as they are today." There is a failure of this nation, its leadership, and people to be the witness in the world their Creator intended. Idolatry and other gross violations of the Torah are given as the reasons. Many commentators, including Fretheim, note the importance of the last phrase "as they are today."[11] This verse is a bridge between what has already happened to God's nation and what is about to happen to all the other nations.

The destruction of Jerusalem and Judah (finishing off the destruction of the northern territories called "Israel") happened. God's own place and people in the world are not spared. There will be a remnant, but their lives as they know them are or will be over. At least according to this verse, this is their reality. Looking back over 2,500 years, the people have continued; the nation's existence has been tenuous at best.

Verse 19 continues the list with an old nemesis and potential ally: "Pharaoh king of Egypt, his servants, his officials, and all his people." The history goes back to Joseph and is well documented in the Torah. To hear a pronouncement of God's judgment on Egypt would be well received *if* not for the previous verse. Egypt might have been an ironic hope to stand militarily against Babylon. The readers of Jeremiah see that hope taken away in this verse. Egypt will also be forced to drink from the cup.

Leadership matters. Jeremiah does not begin with the country but with the leaders—Pharaoh, his servants, his officials, and then, finally, all his peoples. What chance of survival, much less peace, can there be if all of the leaders are drunk? Capitalism and violence are intertwined. Leaders help connect the two. Money can be a kind of "drunkenness" that creates and sustains all sorts

10. Fretheim, *Jeremiah*, 359.

11. Fretheim, *Jeremiah*, 358.

of injustice and evil. The recent conflict in Israel and Gaza gives a modern example. Leaders want to act justly, as do their constituents; however, it comes with a cost. Money talks. Off the record, they were getting calls on a ten to one ratio for an immediate ceasefire in Gaza. Some even stated that what was going on right now was US led. However, they could not act on behalf of their constituents because of the almost certain loss of financial sponsorship that would cost them their jobs.[12] If that cup of wrath is being poured out on the nations today, it is certainly some extremely expensive wine. The behavior could be described as "drunk."

Verse 20 adds to the list "all the mixed people; all the kings of the land of Uz; all the kings of the land of the Philistines—Ashkelon, Gaza, Ekron, and the remnant of Ashdod." The meaning of "the mixed peoples" in this verse is uncertain.[13] It may be like today to refer to peoples who were visiting or had taken up residence in another nation. Considering the history and prominence of Egypt, this is a reasonable explanation. Throughout Scripture and ancient world history, Egypt remained a hub for commerce and civilization. Regardless, they will not miss the cup. All the kings of the land of Uz, once again, highlight leaders as the initial recipients of the cup of wrath. Their "drunken" leadership will trickle down throughout the nation.

Uz is not really known to my commentators. It is mostly known as the home of Job. It is possible Jeremiah, Baruch, or one of their editors was familiar with Job. While pure speculation, this could be an allusion to just how terrible things are going to get. The Philistines are another ancient foe and a neighboring people. According to Lundbom, two of the four cities mentioned, Ashkelon and Ekron, were destroyed by Nebuchadnezzar in 604 BCE.[14] There must have been some hope that other nations would survive and even help Judah against Nebuchadnezzar, but that will not happen.

12. Halper, "Why I Quit," 1:31:01.

13. Lundbom, *Jeremiah 21–36*, 265.

14. Lundbom, *Jeremiah 21–36*, 268.

As the list expands, there is an important theological move. Jeremiah tells the reader that YHWH is sovereign over *all* nations. Can the nations hear that today? It does limit God if it is a "Christian" nation or not. This specific listing of all known nations tells us they all rise and fall at the will of Israel's God.

Verse 21 adds "Edom, Moab, and the Ammonites," all ancient foes and neighbors of Israel. For unclear reasons, the nation, and not the leadership, is named here, though the leadership is probably implied. Once again, these are people to whom Jeremiah has been called to administer the cup of wrath. They are included in the judgment. Jeremiah will mention them again in chapter 49.

Verse 22 returns to highlighting the role of leadership by including "all the kings of Tyre, all the kings of Sidon, and the kings of the coastland across the sea." These were possibly allies participating in the Jerusalem conference of 594 BCE, where rebellion against Babylon was discussed (Jer 27:1–3).[15] Sidon surrendered to Nebuchadnezzar. Tyre underwent a thirteen-year siege before it fell to the same force.[16] It is almost impossible that the kings across the sea were destroyed by Nebuchadnezzar.[17] However, they are mentioned as part of the ongoing theological argument that YHWH is King over all nations.

Verse 23 reverts to talking of nations, rather than leaders: "Dedan, Tema, Buz and all who have shaved temples." Dedan and Tema were caravan centers in Northwest Arabia.[18] The location and history of Buz is unknown; however, it is also mentioned in the book of Job. Elihu is a Buzite. While the biblical scholars do not venture out into this thought, it intrigues me that in these short verses, there are two allusions to Job. While I would not base a sermon on it, the tough theological questions as well as the profound suffering in the book of Job fit well with the cup of wrath. It also lets Satan be the main villain instead of YHWH. A more solid argument can be made that this mystical experience of God passing

15. Lundbom, *Jeremiah 21–36*, 263.
16. Lundbom, *Jeremiah 21–36*, 263.
17. Lundbom, *Jeremiah 21–36*, 263.
18. Lundbom, *Jeremiah 21–36*, 263.

along the cup of wrath to Jeremiah is grounded by mentioning several surrounding nations that existed both in Scripture and in Ancient Near East histories. The mystical took place in specific times and places. Those who have shaved temples are singled out as worthy of the cup. This may have simply been a specific group known to the readers of Jeremiah. The above statement about specifics would apply here. It is odd that there is a move away from both nation and leaders to a group of people identified by their deliberate hair style. Perhaps all means all.

Verse 24 swings back in the direction of leadership with "all the kings of Arabia and all the kings of the mixed peoples that live in the desert." Lundbom notes these are the kings who brought gold to Solomon (1 Kgs 10:14–15) who now are under God's wrath.[19] Perhaps these were long-time friends of Jerusalem after an extensive list of historic enemies. They too must drink from the cup. Included here also is another group of "mixed people," but this time the judgment is directed towards their kings. While there is not consistency, leadership is often mentioned as the beginning of the judgment.

The list moves farther away geographically from Jerusalem as verse 25 adds to the list "all the kings of Zimri, all the kings of Elam, and all the kings of Media."[20] Zimri is unknown, but Elam had been a political force prior to this passage.[21] Media partnered with Babylon to overthrow Nineveh but later was absorbed by the Persians. They had a strong military and political presence in the region. God's sovereignty is expanding and including stronger nations, beginning with their leaders.

Verse 26 concludes the list with "all the kings of the north, far and near, one after another, and all the kingdoms of the world that are on the face of the earth. After them, the king of Sheshach shall drink." None are left out. The LORD sends Jeremiah to every nation on earth, known and unknown, with the cup of wrath. This final statement includes both leadership and people, kings and

19. Lundbom, *Jeremiah 21–36*, 264.

20. Lundbom, *Jeremiah 21–36*, 265.

21. Lundbom, *Jeremiah 21–36*, 265.

kingdoms. Walter Brueggemann says of this entire passage, "It asserts that the entire world of international order is coming unglued, as God has purposed. Every nation will suffer. It is a vision of God's majestic and sovereign power, from which no nation, kingdom, or empire is immune."[22] We might wonder at this point if God is giving up on people or at least organized society. Brueggemann helps again here with an understanding of time. "Forever" is the near future, not timeless.[23] Babylon and its emperor will disorder the ancient world for a lifetime but not forever. This understanding of time is also hopeful for our day. A season of destruction, even near complete destruction, is not forever but for as long as it takes.

Finally, the list concludes: "After them the king of Sheshach shall drink." I am grateful for Bible scholars! All of them noted, with varying amount of detail, that this is a code for Babylon. It is called an *atbush*. The last letter of the Hebrew alphabet is substituted for the first one and so on to spell out this cryptic title for Nebuchadnezzar and his empire. Commentators do not agree on its purpose. Since Babylon is spoken of openly elsewhere, Lundbom offers that it is a wordplay rather than a code.[24] Perhaps it is used to delineate the dual purpose of Babylon and its king.

In his book *Friend or Foe? The Figure of Babylon in the Book of Jeremiah*,[25] John Hill argues that Nebuchadnezzar and the Babylonian Empire serve as both servant and enemy of God's purposes. Like Brueggemann's above understanding of time, there are different seasons—a time for the empire to do God's will and a time for it to also drink the cup of wrath once its service has ended. History may show Babylon is not alone in God's ambivalence towards empire.

Verse 27 provides a summary of the action: "Then you shall say to them, thus says the LORD of hosts, the God of Israel: Drink; get drunk and vomit; fall and rise no more because of the sword that I am sending among you." YHWH is named as well as

22. Brueggemann, *Jeremiah*, 225.

23. Brueggemann, *Jeremiah*, 222.

24. Lundbom, *Jeremiah 21–36*, 266.

25. Hill, *Friend or Foe?*

the specific God of Israel. It is important to note that YHWH is making a claim of sovereignty over all nations. This passage does contain judgment that involves violence, but it is more to do with God's sovereignty than punishment.[26]

What does this say about God? Could we even call this leadership? God has a goal of life over death, of justice, of mercy. The nations fail at this at the same if not greater rate than individuals. Even Israel, who had the plan revealed to them, could not follow it faithfully. Can we call this love? Do the means justify the ends? What does it tell us about God when we see the means (i.e., the drunken, undiscerning sword)? With a lack of cooperation even from God's people, what hope is there to move toward God's goal without an intervention? A wise person will listen to reason. All a fool understands is a stick or a sword (Prov 10:13).

The physical effects of drunkenness are mentioned. There will be a modern comment on vomiting in the excursus. But the effect is thorough. There is a helplessness that comes with excessive drinking and a powerlessness that comes from vomiting as a result of too much drink. But unlike a hangover and a possible next day repentance or swearing off, this consequence is death.

Fall and rise no more seems to not be hyperbole. While it could be debated, the promise that these nations would fall and rise no more holds mostly true 2,500 years later. What is left of Israel would fall at the hand of Nebuchadnezzar in 586 BCE, its autonomy destroyed. While it is debatable, even to today, it can be seen as a vassal state to various empires. As for the other kingdoms, Saddam Hussein made a short attempt at restoring Babylon. Egypt has continued but far from the empire it once was.

Verse 28 falls back into a kind of mysticism (if the passage ever left it behind) in that God is giving this order to Jeremiah without any concrete way of conveying the order: "And if they refuse to accept the cup from your hand to drink, then you shall say to them: Thus says the LORD of hosts: You must drink!" There is no record of Jeremiah traveling to these nations. And yet, God

26. Brueggemann, *Jeremiah*, 222.

chooses to give this order to the prophet to the nations. It is a second order alongside verse 15. All nations have been judged.

Thinking about global trade, travel, and political friends and foes, it would make little sense that only some of the nations would be involved in this judgment. It would be a stretch to claim that any were "innocent."

Verse 29 concludes the passage: "See, I am beginning to bring disaster to the city that is called by my name, and how can you avoid punishment? You shall not go unpunished, for I am summoning a sword against all the inhabitants of the earth, says the LORD of hosts." This may clarify some sort of rationale for YHWH's judgment. Judah has been prosecuted for twenty-five chapters. If the city/people/nation that God loves is to be destroyed, why would any be spared? All have sinned, and all are interconnected.

This passage serves several purposes. It reveals that the God of Judah and Jerusalem are both the God of all nations. Many commentators note this is the primary interpretation of this passage. Second, it underlines Jeremiah's calling as prophet to all nations, not just his people. Third, it raises a few theological issues that will be discussed below, such as what we can learn about the character of God and how the All Merciful can also be the One who brings violence to all peoples.

A BIRTH OF VIOLENCE THROUGH A THEOLOGY OF RACE

Idolatry leads away from God's will being done on earth as it is in heaven. One of the most consequential effects of idolatry is violence. One trajectory of violence that is still prevalent today is caused by racism. In his book *The Christian Imagination: Theology and the Origins of Race*,[27] Willie James Jennings argues that western colonialism and Christian evangelism are joined in an unholy, idolatrous way. The acquisition of land and the enslavement of peoples walked hand in hand with a sincere desire to convert

27. Jennings, *Christian Imagination.*

them to Christianity. This resulted in the creation of the spectrum of race alongside changing the role of humans from steward to owner of land. Race and private property are two sides of the same coin, and those who created the situation believed they were doing so at the direction of God. Colonialism, and all that came with it, is rooted in a distorted, idolatrous action justified under "God's Providence."[28] Jennings's critique of the church, our complicity with the sin of colonialism, and the violence that came with it will be explored here, along with the continuing trajectory of those forms of idolatry in the US.

Providential Theology: Racism, Colonialism, and Violence in the Name of God

Jennings reveals a theological history that helps explain the idolatry that is formed by the relationship between racism, colonialism, and violence:

> Prince Henry, following his deepest Christian instincts, ordered a tithe be given to God through the church. Two black boys were given, one to the principal church in Lagos and another to the Franciscan convent on Cape Saint Vincent. This act of praise and thanksgiving to God for allowing Portugal's successful entrance into maritime power also served to justify the royal rhetoric by which Prince Henry claimed his motivation was the salvation of the soul of the heathen.[29]

This quote nicely sums up the partnership formed by this idolatry. Like Rockefeller's claim discussed in chapter 1 that "God gave me this money," the enslavement of other human beings using evangelism as sincere theological cover reveals a result when a god different from the one revealed to us through Israel and later through the Messiah is followed. The beginnings of the horrors of coercive violence are narrated through the separation of families:

28. Jennings, *Christian Imagination*, 92

29. Jennings, *Christian Imagination*, 16.

> For as often as they had placed them in one part the sons, seeing their fathers in another, rose with great energy and rushed over to them; the mothers clasped their other children in their arms, and threw themselves flat on the ground with them; receiving blows with little pity for their own flesh, if only they might not be torn from them. And so troublously they finished the partition.[30]

The practice of family separation was not the first nor the last. It's current practice among immigrant families is either based on dehumanization or reliance on short memories that move on every few news cycles.

The theft of the land was justified by claiming God's providence as well as racial superiority. Jennings narrates the challenges of this in his chapter on Bishop John Colenso, who had before him the task of "grasping both the inner logics of Christian theology and inner native logics. This was beyond his ability."[31] A separate way of saying this comes from Acosta, who understood his working coming from a "loving Christian service. Theology would stand over native flesh calling the natives to a higher form of life."[32] This "higher form of life" will require a theological shift from being stewards of God's creation to being lords over private property.

It is hard to fathom how a Christianity could arise that could not see the evil in this, and yet we cannot look at the speck in our ancestors' eyes and ignore the plank in our own. It is hard to fathom how any baptized person, filled with the Holy Spirit and tasked with bearing witness to the kingdom of God, could find themselves engaged with this activity then or now. And yet, here it is. This small illustration of kidnapping and family separation repeats itself, and much worse, hundreds of thousands of times over the next four hundred years. Claiming God's sovereignty over the African and Native American peoples, violence became a means. While Jesus overcomes death, enslaved peoples are killed and have

30. Jennings, *Christian Imagination*, 19.

31. Jennings, *Christian Imagination*, 149.

32. Jennings, *Christian Imagination*, 105.

death used as a threat to subdue them.[33] It is the opposite of the faithful Christian witness.

The Trajectory of Racism and Christianity in the US

Jennings notes how this "providential" theology led to the taking of the lands of what was called "the New World." In one interview,[34] he invites us to imagine the Europeans landing on the shores of North America. For the first time, they see this new world. From the Shenandoah Valley to the Great Lakes to the Rocky Mountains, a voice that they believed to be God said, "It's all yours!"[35] Jennings notes, "It is a truism to say that humans are bound to the earth. However, that articulated connection to the earth comes under profound and devastating alteration with the age of discovery and colonialism."[36] Jennings goes on to describe the Native American belief and practice that humans and animals were intimately connected. The introduction of the idea of "private property" diverged from this connectedness to the point that the colonizers had to destroy the original inhabitants. The two views of land and all that is in it are incompatible.[37]

This idolatrous theology continued into the history of the US, as outlined in Kelly Baker's *Gospel According to the Klan: The KKK's Appeal to Protestant America, 1915–1930.*[38] Understandings of both race and justifications for colonialism each evolved. Blunt dehumanization began to be questioned. It still existed but became more subtle. Baker argues that the resurgence of the Klan during this period was a process of rebranding. It was no longer a continuation of the Civil War. It was a reenvisioned "get behind Old Glory and the Church of Jesus Christ."[39] This rebranding con-

33. Jennings, *Christian Imagination*, 21.
34. Jennings, "Willie James Jennings Workshops," 2:50:33.
35. Camp, "Christian Imagination," 52:16.
36. Jennings, *Christian Imagination*, 40.
37. Jennings, *Christian Imagination*, 48.
38. Baker, *Gospel According to the Klan*.
39. Baker, *Gospel According to the Klan*, 1.

cealed, at least partially, the reality of violence inflicted on any who found themselves outside of a specific vision of a white Christian nation. Baker narrates the new beginnings of the Klan with the story of a Georgia lynching of Leo Frank, a Northern Jew. A local newspaper described the lynching: the crunching of flesh.[40] In an interview with Lee Camp, Jennings said the Klan is simply a natural outgrowth of the theology revealed in his book.[41]

Both progressives and conservatives condemn the Klan. However, Baker notes that "its numerical strength and popularity require a reevaluation of the order and its place in our narratives to see how such a movement fits within our tellings and retellings of American history, especially American religious history."[42] Baker also mentions the Klan's allegiance to the Protestant Reformation.[43] The emphasis on the Bible and personal salvation kept the door open to perverse interpretations of community. With a theological emphasis away from community and toward individual salvation as primary helped create an injustice that has yet to be righted. With the separation of churches according to race, it allowed both the salvation of individual souls alongside the scale of "white" being near perfection and "black" near lostness.[44] This theological error has led to violence and its justification. If America is God's kingdom or one day will be, then whatever America does must be God's will.

Baker goes on to ask some engaging questions:

> How might narrative of American religious history be told if the Klan was integrated rather than segregated? If a white supremacist movement proves pivotal rather than fringe, then what might happen to our narratives of nation? Would American religious history appear differently, or would it stay shockingly similar? By inserting the Klan into narratives of American religious history,

40. Baker, *Gospel According to the Klan*, 2–3.
41. Camp, "Christian Imagination."
42. Baker, *Gospel According to the Klan*, 10.
43. Baker, *Gospel According to the Klan*, 87.
44. Jennings, *Christian Imagination*, 24.

> the relationship between faith and nationalism comes to the foreground.[45]

Combined with a conversation around private property, we begin to see it is less about a political category and more about the water we swim in. The commodification of resources is a reality shared by most if not all Americans. Condemning the more extreme expressions of that, such as the Klan, simply puts us in a different place on Cavanaugh's scale of idolatry.[46] It is not bowing down to a gold covered statue, but it is about the latest purchase from Amazon with little care about how that order was "fulfilled."

Unchecked, this theological trajectory that distinguishes humans, including baptized Christians, as lesser or greater based mostly on skin color and quickly shifting to economic worth infiltrates society to its core. Joe Moore with Jon Land shares his story as an undercover KKK informant in *White Robes and Broken Badges.*[47] Moore details not only the current organization of the Klan but also some level of membership of local law enforcement. He also mentions other white supremacist groups that were more prominent in the January 6, 2021, incident in Washington, DC. Their presence and empowerment continue today in a race that is over and done. God's providence and the violence to back it up remain at the forefront. The cup of wrath is still being drunk, especially among the leaders. But is this God pouring out the cup or the continued captivity of the church to an idol? Is this simply our human sinfulness, or is this God building a case against a nation? Is God about to be sorry that America was made?

HOW DID WHITE PEOPLE BECOME SUPREME?

Another serious theological error called supersessionism is a primary theme of Jennings' work and deeply implicated in the

45. Baker, *Gospel According to the Klan*, 19.

46. Cavanaugh, email correspondence regarding *The Uses of Idolatry*, May 15, 2024.

47. Moore and Land, *White Robes and Broken Badges*.

idolatry at the heart of these issues of racism, colonialism, and violence in the United States. Supersessionism is the theological move to replace Israel with white Christians. Christians, using a particular interpretation of Paul and Hebrews (and, to a lesser degree, the Gospels),[48] claimed to replace Israel as the people of God. Once this occurred, the church was "free" to do whatever it wanted and justify it as "God's providential will."[49] This idolatry, which abandoned much of Jesus' teaching regarding loving neighbor and enemy, led to a violent church. Each nation that claimed Jesus as Lord came to think of itself as God's chosen people.[50] Jennings gives an outstanding example of the great hymn writer, Isaac Watts, who rewrote the Psalms with England in the place of Israel.[51] In addition to the enslavement and stealing of a third of the world's land, it gave birth to nationalism and led to the Shoah.

It is the coercive connection of the commodification of creation and an idolatrous movement of the gospel into the "New World" that stands at the base of violence. The fruit of that idolatry (clearly seen in Gaza from 2023 through the time of this writing in 2025, as well as random mass murders in America) is a world able to quickly annihilate itself via nuclear weapons. An equal but slower threat is climate collapse. There is a large body of theological and scientific work regarding that future.[52] Both begin with certain nations claiming to be Lord. Some invoke Jesus, others do not. The behavior is an attempt to supplant God. The nations, or at least enough of them, have reclaimed the sin of Gen 3:14. They (we) want to be God.

While Jer 25:15–29 does not lay the sin of idolatry upon all the nations, Israel is certainly accused of it throughout the first twenty-five chapters. It is not a bold move to, likewise, accuse any nation today claiming to be Christian of this sin when they act as their own god. This presents us with the probability of God's

48. Jennings, *Christian Imagination*, 155.

49. Jennings, *Christian Imagination*, 276.

50. Jennings, *Christian Imagination*, 155.

51. Jennings, *Christian Imagination*, 211–12.

52. See Norman Wirzba, Wendell Berry, and Ched Myers, among others.

judgment once again coming upon not only Israel but all nations. There is a significant difference, however. Idols today—such as weapons, fossil fuels, and white Christian nationalism—are very capable of causing much death. We have the power to extinguish ourselves.

While any attempts at justification will be inadequate, the need for God to claim and even exert (even through violence) sovereignty over the nations toward life, instead of death, is justified at least as a temporary means. In other words, God is always moving creation and all that is with it, including the nations, toward life. Sometimes dead or nearly dead branches, even whole trees, need cutting. That work can be seen in Scripture with Israel, Babylon, and others. It can be seen in more current times with nations, including America. Jeremiah explores, in chapters 29 through 31, what a more permanent cooperation between God, humanity, and the nations will be. But chapter 25 leaves us wrestling with the reality that God obviously allows violence and may, on occasion, use it to an end—The End—when death will be no more.

In Jer 25:15–29 as well as other places in his testimony, we witness God wiping out the nations. It is not a complete end to the nations, but it is a level of destruction that leads to a decision. There will be either an abandonment of the nation's former glory or a rebuild into something new. When we think of Rome, Italy, or Athens, Greece, today, we see functional cities and nations that seem to share little in common with the history of empire. However, in large swaths of history, these cities and peoples ruled much of the known world. The same could be said of Tokyo, Japan, Berlin, Germany, and even London, England. These nations and peoples briefly held much worldly power. Isaac Watts would have a challenge justifying his rewrites today. There is not much left of the British Empire. The heart of this thesis is to provide an exploration of a possible, if not probable, future of this happening to the United States of America.

The move from being steward of the land to the commodification of all that was encountered (land, animals, peoples) initiated a level of violence that has now led to the possible extinction of humanity. It has already led to the extinction of thousands of animals as well as the extensive pollution of all that is needed for life. In an interview about his book *The Christian Imagination*, Jennings said that race and acquisition of the land are two sides of the same coin.[53] Mixing that with the eternal growth model of capitalism, it is only a matter of time before the planet is uninhabitable to humans and much of the rest of God's creation as a burgeoning and evermore rapacious humanity overwhelms all creation. The Creator, Savior, and Sustainer has been traded in for a white colonialist god who has claimed the United States of America (and other places under its influence) as the new Jerusalem and its authority as the kingdom of God. It will defend that position with as much violence as necessary. Underneath the religious veneer is voracious capitalism. It is proving to be insatiable.

So, in addition to the violence rooted in white supremacy, we have an even more destructive violence rooted in capitalism's conversion of creation into a commodity. As European Christians divorced themselves first from Israel (a move back toward Marcionism) then from other peoples, an economic system capable of consuming creation was born. This idol was discussed thoroughly in chapter 1 of this work. Its link with race and Christian providence breathe power into its gold and silver. This theological error allowed them and us as their religious descendants to claim God's gift of creation as our own. And we are continuing down this path of self-destruction.

The difficulty in claiming responsibility for violence by Christians today is an inability to see the truth in Jennings' work. The current debate in Christian discipleship that is intermingled with its relationship with America seems to cast in "liberal" and "conservative" labels with the Klan often described as part of the "fringe right." None of this gets to the root Jennings exposes. Whether Christians claim violence in self-defense or in the "renewal" of America via repression of migrants and the continued repression of people of color regardless of national origins, violence is consistently available as a means—often as a preferred

53. Camp, "Christian Imagination."

means. Violence is the opposite of peace. The will of God will be brought to God's creation via the cross, not the sword. However, our Scripture reveals moments of God acting violently, which I will discuss below in an excursus on a mystical dimension of God's character focusing on suffering, violence, and sovereignty.

Jennings helps us see a significant part of how we got to where we are—"we" being a church that rarely makes a distinction between being a Christian and being an American. Just to ask if there is a difference between being an American and a Christian creates confusion in many of those I pastor. The cup of wrath was God's answer to nations gone awry over 2,500 years ago. If the world is on the verge of that happening again, we will find out what cross carrying is about. But no matter what happens, we do not live as those who have no hope. The gospel has the final word.

THE TRUE GOD ACTS—A SERMON ON JEREMIAH 25:15–29 AND REVELATION 7:9

What happens when the God we are worshiping and trying to emulate is a false one? As we explored in the previous sermon, idolatry is a prevalent temptation in Jeremiah's Israel and seems obvious to us today. One of the most obvious consequences of our idolatry is violence. When we are justifying and sometimes even directly participating in violence "in God's name," we can be sure we are lost. We have bowed before an idol.

In our lessons today, we see God's response. It is a hard reset. But it is not the end. Truthfully, there is worse to come. But we have a God, sooner or later, who acts towards God's ends, which is peace on earth, goodwill to all.

Jeremiah 25:15–29 is scary. In the first twenty-five chapters of Jeremiah, we hear the warnings. We have reshaped and even broken pottery in chapter 18. We have good and bad figs in chapter 24. All of these are mixed with a call for the leaders and the people to repent, to return to the God of Abraham, Isaac, and Jacob, to return to the covenant given to Moses. But when we get to today, it is too late. God acts.

> For thus the LORD, the God of Israel, said to me: "Take from my hand this cup of the wine of wrath, and make all the nations to whom I send you drink it." They shall drink and stagger and go out of their minds because of the sword that I am sending among them. (25:15–16)

Have you ever been around a drunk? It is used to explain a lot of abhorrent behavior. It produces a temporary insanity that can, and usually does, have all sorts of destructive, less temporary effects. Jails, institutions, and even cemeteries have plenty of testimonies about those who have had "one too many."

Today, God and Jeremiah use this image to try and explain to us in a way we can understand what happens when God needs to reset, when God needs to judge that which is not useful and see what is left.

Old Testament scholars have been hard pressed to explain what is literally happening here. We are not sure if Jeremiah had a vision or a dream. We are not sure how Jeremiah could preach to these nations, much less make them drink from this cup of wrath. I mention this because these are not good questions. What we can say for sure is that God oversees the nations, and their usefulness to God's will being done on earth as it is in heaven has ended. The LORD is King.

What does this tell us about God? Christians fall into idolatry and the heresy that comes with it when we talk about the God of the Old Testament, a God of wrath, and the God of the New Testament, a God of love. Walter Brueggemann argues in his book *Theology of the Old Testament* that there is a complex revelation of God in the Old Testament. The primary testimony is a God who loves God's people and God's creation—a God who blesses all through Israel with directions and care. There is another secondary testimony that we find in places like Job and our lesson today where God does not seem to act in love nor care. It is wrath. It is throwing away and starting over. Lest we think Jesus is not capable of this, I refer us to Matt 25:31–46 where he, very similarly to our lesson today, judges the nations of the world. Those nations that care for the least of these will enter eternal life, and those who do not care for the least of these will "depart from me into the eternal fire prepared for the devil and his angels."

We preachers and theologians try to figure this out. One truth is that God is God, and we are not. The other truth is that God is sovereign over all of God's creation, including the nations, as revealed in our lesson today. We can debate about promises and covenants and God's character revealed in that. But the bottom line is God is free to do whatever God wants with it all.

And today God is throwing in the towel. The end begins with God's people: "Jerusalem and the towns of Judah, its kings and officials, to make them a desolation and a waste, an object of hissing and of cursing, as they are today" (25:18). This we have seen coming for twenty-five chapters. But it is still harsh. It has already happened. While we will look at this more closely in our following sermon, we know that Jerusalem was destroyed by Babylon and its leader Nebuchadnezzar around 586 BCE. God's witness on earth has failed.

Why God extends this drunken wrath onto all the other nations is a bit more mysterious. We are not given a "why" like we have with Israel. What we do see is that God is Lord and judge over all the nations and peoples. If we need a why, it is laid out in Matt 25:31–46. God has a plan for God's creation. Some people follow that better than others.

God and Jeremiah move the cup from Jerusalem and Judah to Egypt, then to a thorough list of nations that do not exist today, then finally to the empire of that time, Babylon, oddly referred to in a Hebrew code name, *Sheshach*. It is Babylon spelled backwards. While this could have been meant as a secret, a more likely motive was poking a bit of mockery at the empire.

We know from the history books that all of this happened. There was a taking away of power at least and an end in some cases. Anyone met a Philistine lately? But you may even have a neighbor today from Egypt. Some nations made it into the modern world and some did not.

That truth brings us to our good news today. Revelation 7:9 gives us a vision of where all of this is heading: "After this I looked, and there was a great multitude that no one could count, from every nation, from all tribes and peoples and languages, standing before the throne and before the Lamb." This is part of the vision of where God is taking God's creation and all that is in it. The time of one nation or people having power over another will be gone. We will stand together as both God's friends and children, not one above another.

What does any of this have to do with us? Willie Jennings, in his book *The Christian Imagination: Theology and the Origins of Race*, traces the invention of race and its consequences. Several theological moves were made by European Christians that resulted in them justifying the stealing of two continents worth of land and four hundred years of labor as the will of God. While Jennings does not focus on the violence present in all of this, it is well documented throughout this history even to the present day. Under the umbrella of "white supremacy," grabs for power continued and seemed to become more desperate as God moved the kingdom forward.

Yet, the false idol of a "white" god or savior could be abandoned. If the church in this country could catch a vision of Rev 7:9, it might help us repent. As it stands today, this vision remains a blur while we instead engage in some sort of nostalgic fiction of a better time that could all be brought back with prayer in schools, or as I have heard it, if we could go back to a time when "people knew their place."

A few days ago, I was about to park at our local Walmart. I saw a black man standing in the lot looking my way, and a dose of fear hit me. I am not sure where it came from. Jennings would argue it came from five hundred years of people moving in the opposite direction of God's will. Fear is the fruit of that movement. But I had been listening to one of his interviews, and I asked myself, "What would Willie do?" I parked the car, got out, and the man and I made eye contact. I am not sure who spoke first, but in a few moments, we were walking along together toward the store laughing aloud. I found out we had something important in common: we both hated Walmart! We parted company in the store and then saw each other in the parking lot again. This time I rolled down my window and waved. "Did you get those headlight bulbs?" he shouted. "Yeah, did you get your stuff?" I replied. "Yeah." "Great," I said. "Take it easy out there!" "You, too!"

It was not much. But for a moment, the cup of wrath was put aside for two people from two different cultures acting as friends. I am sure we would be grateful to see each other gathered around the throne someday.

Sadly, Jeremiah shows us the great suffering that Rev 7:14b describes as the mass of humanity "who have come out of the great ordeal." There is a cross-carrying suffering to come before the great celebration. Death precedes resurrection. Almost all will be lost to get to that glorious time. We will look at that in the next sermon.

EXCURSUS: A MYSTICAL WITNESS

Before heading into a discussion in the next chapter on the probable death of an empire, it is appropriate to take a moment to reflect on my understanding of the character of God and how that has developed over my lifetime. Christian mysticism has a broad and long history. Below are several encounters I have had over about a twenty-year period. I conclude by discussing how I see them as relating to the character of God.

When I was almost twenty years old, I had a dream. The photo I kept of the white Euro-American version of Jesus on my bedstand transformed into an encounter with the living Christ. We were sitting across from one another at a table. The "Hallelujah Chorus" was playing very loudly. He put a finger to his lips and the music quieted but could still be heard. I held my right hand toward him, and he had a ring. He tried putting it on my forefinger, but it stung so badly that I pulled my hand away. It felt like the ring was lined with sharp needles. Then he tried putting it on my middle finger. The same feeling elicited the same reaction from me. The ring finger was also the same. As he held the ring out over my pinkie, he looked at me. I wanted the ring. I knew if I trusted him, he would be able to put it on. And he did. I was surprised that blood did not cover my finger. Instead, a light green glow came from the stone of the ring and filled the room. I remember looking in a corner. No shadow. In another scene, he finally spoke: "You are weak, and you must be strong."

When I woke up, my mother met me downstairs. As I told her about this, I remember the ends of my fingers still hurt. When I think about it now, forty years later, the pinkie still does.

The next encounter happened about two years later. I was asleep but the scene was in my room. There was a young person in a white robe sitting on a shelf near the window. He told me that he was a collector of souls. I asked him what his name was. He said, "My name is . . . and the light switch made a sound like being turned on." And I woke up. I named him Click, and in my mind's eye I can still see him sitting there.

Another couple of years passed. This story requires a bit of history. My friend had a dream of Jesus hanging on the cross and thought that it should be him instead of Jesus. I remember thinking that I did not have that much conviction of my sin. That night in a dream, I was standing in line, and the same Euro-American version of Jesus was coming down the line serving communion. He had on a white robe and a short, gold colored stole. When he got to me, I held out my hands to receive the bread and said, "I love you, man." And he looked back at me, deep into me and said, "Except for that first Thursday." And I woke up. I knew and still know I would have abandoned him, too.

A couple of years after that, when I was about twenty-five, I was once again dreaming. The scene was up in an airplane. There were no seats; I was standing looking out the window. A bright light filled the window, and a luminous human being appeared in front of me. He/She held a rectangular container about four inches by five inches and about an inch deep. It was filled with a light brown substance that looked like vomit. While I was looking at it, the being said, "This is what America has ordered, but yet to receive."

Sometime close to this, I had another dream. I was looking at a person sitting on a park-style bench. He looked very sophisticated and well dressed in a black coat with a white shirt. He was staring out ahead. Something inside me said, this is Satan. The scene changed, and I was in a bedroom. Things were flying about like a whirlwind. Lamps, furniture. I kept trying to duck. I looked down, and there was a small being covered in light brown hair. It was a foot tall with piercing eyes. I can still see the eyes. Something told me, this is God the Father. A little hand came out under the hair and pointed toward a door. I walked in, and it was complete, silent darkness. No light. And I woke up.

In another dream, around this time, I was looking at a pool of water created by a waterfall. The most beautiful being I have ever seen emerged. I cannot really describe it. There was something like fish scales, but they were glimmering. And he/she/they emerged out of the pool. I was overwhelmed by the beauty. Something told me, this is the new creature. I remember saying, "So you have the body of a fish and the mind of God?" And he/she/they said, "Yes."

In 1997, when I was thirty-three, I was trying to discern a call to campus ministry. But I knew I was about to derail a fast-tracking career that may one day result in pastoring a large congregation. But the whole reason I wanted to go into the ministry was to work at a university as a pastor. I was praying and asking God for help with this decision when the Euro-American version of Jesus briefly appeared in my office and said, "Go." I sat there and wept. And I got the job for six years.

During that time, I was meeting with a spiritual director, Don Kelley. I was trying to discern purchasing a motorcycle. Don had given me a process to discern God's will on this issue. Leaving his office, I was driving up the highway when I fell into a bit of trance. A voice said deep inside me, "I want you to buy the bike and learn how to ride it well." There were a couple of second pauses. Then, "How's that for a discernment process."

Due to several circumstances, I was asked to leave the campus ministry position. I was heartbroken. I rode my motorcycle up to the Blue Ridge Parkway, parked, and started praying. By this time, I had a spouse, two small children, and a home. I had lost my dream job and my primary reason for entering the ministry. I fell into another trance. The voice inside me asked, "Rich, do you believe I made all this?" I looked out over those mountains that went on for as far as I could see, and I knew they had been there a long time. "Yes, Lord, I do." Once again, a couple of seconds pause. "Do you think I could take care of you?"

As a Methodist, I could not do much theology without appealing to my personal experience. All the above occurred over a twenty-year period. I have had some other experiences but none as profound. For me, what they reveal about this character of God is multifaceted. First, Jesus is alive! I have seen him and spoken with him on more than one occasion. Second, my calling has and will involve pain. Third, this God has cared for me through quite a bit. Fourth, there is a mysterious part of my calling that is yet to be revealed. The motorcycle discernment is one of those odd portions that simply makes little sense now or over the years.

There is also implied violence in these dreams—some of it directed at me! This raises some challenging questions about God's character. I once shared the vomit story with a group of ministers, and one shouted out, "No!" He would not accept that this dream came from God. And yet, we have Scripture filled with human failure, with principalities and powers failing to move toward God's will for earth. Is not some sort of judgment, some sort of coercion inevitable? Jeremiah 25:15–29 is a witness to this inevitability, and yet it is shrouded in mystical vision—e.g., "the cup of wrath."

In the book *Violence in Scripture*,[54] Jerome Creach surveys passages that contribute to this conversation. After reading this book, one interpretation of the Jeremiah passage is God *allowing* human activity to act as it does, often violently. This is especially true of empires, including Babylon and America. They are allowed a season to bring violence and then they are either reduced in power or destroyed.

We can see this in Rome, Greece, Britain. These nations still exist but not as "empires." In the dream of the vomit, America has evidently "ordered" that; it is not a violent threat from God but a delivery of reaping what a nation sows. Given the horrific violence

54. Creach, *Violence in Scripture*.

we have seen these last few years just inside the borders of this country, alongside the funding of the genocide currently being committed by the modern nation state of Israel, we must wonder if the glass case is near opening or has already.

While a detailed summary of Creach's work is beyond this thesis, I must say he does a thorough job "softening" any violence that could be blamed on God through a close reading of Scripture and historical circumstances. This does not explain all of it, but most. Adding Brueggemann's understanding of the secondary testimony in Scripture, and the burden of proof lies on those who believe in a wrathful God. While we must not fall into the heresy of Marcion, Christians do believe that Jesus' birth, life, death, resurrection, and ascension is a full revelation of God and God's will. Jesus renounced violence in thought, word, and deed. However, he did leave open the possibility of reaping what we sow: "Those that live by the sword will die by it" (Matt 26:52).

It is hard to overstate how much Jeremiah suffered, physically, emotionally, and spiritually. He earned the nickname, "the weeping prophet." Much of my interest in this book is to try and make sense of my calling. I would be hard pressed to call it "suffering" at this point.

Finally, it seems possible that God could care for us as individuals *and* judge our idolatries, especially those connected to worshiping nations and economic systems. The question that I have for my calling, and all these dreams that do not seem too far from other witnesses in Scripture, is what sort of leadership I need to develop to walk into whatever God is doing here. There is little question about the violence around me. There are enough weapons within a one-mile radius to arm a small army. That God is encouraging the followers of Jesus to arm ourselves seems a hard "No!" to me. It is a denial of the resurrection and, in some ways, a failure to carry the cross.

CONCLUSION

I have been taught that leadership is as much about asking the right questions as it is about having answers. I have only scratched the surface, but I hope I asked questions that will at least give pause to many assumptions among the people I pastor, namely, that our actions as a people regarding our relationship with violence has little to do with us. We rely on violence as yet another false god. It is tied into the identity of America, to our economic system, and, sadly, the fabric of the church. It is likely we are only at the beginning of what is to come. Jeremiah saw the destruction of his nation and religion. It could have ended the people appointed to be God's blessing in the world. The church and America stand in a similar time. Next, we look in the tomb.

CHAPTER 3

INTO THE DARKNESS

Many Christians are in a desperate time of looking for direction from anyone or just checking out altogether, either from church, society, or life. I am trying to say that with hope. This essay is mostly for my fellow Christians who also claim America as a home and identity. They (we), perhaps to a degree beyond what I believe, are lost.

Below, I argue two things. First, the book of Jeremiah illustrates that God's people have survived the death of a nation and empire. Second, that death re-centered their hope in the God who called them to be a people. Since the church in America finds itself in such a time, we can find hope and truth in the words of Jeremiah. Today, Christians living in America can find hope and truth in the words, "Jesus is Lord." One way to look at this invitation is to believe that something or someone is going to be Lord, or claim that role. In chapters 1 and 2, I have argued that idolatry and its fruit, violence, have claimed lordship over many. In important ways, the idolatry of *mammon* and the violence that have proceeded from it define America. Even worse, idolatry and violence have been done "in the name of Jesus." However, God is still at work. A new heaven and a new earth have been promised in Rev 21. What remains to be seen is how much, if any, of this one will be left.

EXEGESIS OF JEREMIAH 51:1–10 (IN CONVERSATION WITH CHAPTERS 46–51)

Jeremiah, chapters 46 through 51, describe the judgment that is visited on the nations. Jeremiah is more than a prophet to Judah. He has been appointed as a prophet to the nations (1:5b). This judgment was predicted in chapter 25, and in chapters 46 through 51, it is about to happen. Depending on one's perspective, the harshest judgment or fairest justice is saved for the Babylonian Empire. Chapters 50 and 51 detail its destruction. The heart of those two chapters is a poem, 51:1–10, and is exegeted below.

Verse 1 begins, "Thus says the LORD: I am going to stir up a destructive wind against Babylon and against the inhabitants of Leb-qamai," God is speaking the destructive wind into action. Each possibility of the intended audience for his speech creates a different anticipation. For Jeremiah and for the modern reader, this is a major shift.[1] Babylon has been the ally/tool of the LORD to bring God's judgment/justice on to God's people. Now it is Babylon's turn. For the exiles, this announcement might get a "*finally*!" response. They have lost everything but their lives because of this enemy. It is good news to hear God is going to act. How Babylonians might have heard these words is hard to say. It could be like today's end of the world "prophets," some of whom have been very financially successful in their predictions of doom but are ignored by many people and the political leadership. True prophets and false ones have all contributed to dark predictions. David Jeremiah is a popular "rapture" televangelist who grabs a lot of airtime around here. There is an overwhelming tone to this prophecy, however. There is also an intermingling of the fate of Judah and the nations. Likewise, God's sovereignty can be claimed over America, the church in America, and all other nations.

This essay was written about a month after Hurricane Helene came through our region. Its destruction raises theological questions. Why did this happen? Again, it depends on whom you speak to. Many will rightly claim this is a consequence of global

1. Brueggemann, *Jeremiah*, 462.

warming. Hurricanes have a purpose: to cool land and water. Others, perhaps in line with Jeremiah here, see this as an instrument of God's wrath. Given whom I have seen affected by this, it is a blunt instrument if this is true. There was little or no distinction between the "righteous" and "unrighteous," but some speculated, even stated as fact, why God judged some but not others. It could be asked if all Babylonians "deserved" the destruction of their empire, nation, people, way of life. While this outcome is not included in our passage, it has been obvious Helene provided a beautiful opportunity to love our neighbors as ourselves. There has been a great generosity of giving and receiving that continues to be an outcome of this storm. Perhaps the same happened in Babylon. While it is vital to distinguish between questions of theodicy and empire, we see in Jeremiah a blending. The God of the wind and sea is also Lord of the nations. God brings order, or reorder, in ways that are often questionable, but Jeremiah points toward God's lordship of all of creation, storms and nations included.

All speculation aside, Jeremiah is clear. This destructive wind is coming from YHWH. It is against both the empire and the people living in it. Perhaps there is an openness to interpretation, including the above reflection, when focusing on the term "Leb-qamai." This is a code for Chaldeans or Babylonians. There is some debate about why it is used here.[2] Terence Fretheim ties the code to the broader theme: "In Hebrew the words Leb-qamai mean 'the heart of those who rise up against me,' picking up themes of arrogance and rebellion."[3] This use of code may be an attempt by Jeremiah to introduce some level of mystery and uncertainty to this judgment. In other words, some living in Babylon may escape the coming destructive wind, but the Leb-qamai will not—perhaps an important distinction given the diversity of the church today, and especially when trying to understand why some suffer more than others.

Verse 2 reads, "And I will send winnowers to Babylon, and they shall winnow her. They shall empty her land when they come

2. Lundbom, *Jeremiah 37–52*, 432.

3. Fretheim, *Jeremiah*, 634.

against her from every side on the day of trouble." Similarly to the mysteries found in verse 1, winnowing and a destructive wind are incompatible.[4] Winnowing, or the practice of separating wheat from chaff, requires a breeze, not a wind capable of destruction. Jeremiah's use of this image implies some discernment. While God is capable of complete destruction of Babylon, winnowing implies a judgment between that which God wished to destroy and that which is still useful to God's will.

This verse also begins to answer why Babylon has come under YHWH's judgment or justice. Just as Babylon was sent by God to winnow, if not destroy, Judah, so others are coming to do the same to Babylon. This theme underpins chapters 50 and 51 and the entire book of Jeremiah. YHWH is sovereign over all nations, not just Judah. Babylon was an instrument to bring God's wrath, or judgment, or justice to Judah. Now their time has come. Babylon has overstepped its bounds, and it is no longer a servant of YHWH but an enemy.[5] The reason for the judgment is a common one: pride. Jeremiah 50:31–32 states,

> I am against you, O arrogant one, says the LORD of hosts, for your day has come, the time when I will punish you. The arrogant one shall stumble and fall, with no one to raise him up, and I will kindle a fire in his cities, and it will devour everything around him.

Babylon was once an ally, but its success in Judah and other nations has led to a pride that is incompatible with God's plans for the nations. Perhaps that will be amended by some winnowing, or perhaps it will require more extreme measures. The second half of 51:2 implies it will be the latter: "They shall empty her land." Babylon will have done to it what it did to Judah.[6] Once again, the underlying point is that YHWH is Lord and not Babylon,

4. Lundbom, *Jeremiah 37–52*, 432.
5. Varughese and Modine, *Jeremiah 26–52*, 296.
6. Lundbom, *Jeremiah 37–52*, 366.

Nebuchadnezzar, nor even, in an extra insult, the gods Bel and Merodach.[7] YHWH is staking a claim here.

Verse 3 continues, "Let not the archer bend his bow and let him not array himself in his coat of mail. Do not spare her young men; utterly destroy her entire army." There are some questions as to whom this command is addressed.[8] If it is to the Babylonian army, there is an implied uselessness to fighting back against the "winnowers." The outcome has already been decided. If it is a command to the winnowers, those who come against Babylon from all sides on the day of trouble, then we have a more nuanced command. The desired outcome will be accomplished by unusual means. There is no need to prepare for war either by offense or defense (arraignment in coat of mail); God will craft the destruction. YHWH will be the sole victor.[9]

The outcome is still the same. Either by destructive "natural" means, or invading armies, or by surrender, Babylon's ability to dominate and even defend itself is being taken away. Cyrus overtook Babylon with little conflict. History shows it was more of a surrender than utter destruction.[10] The same end was accomplished. Babylon as a powerful empire is no more. When we think of Rome, Athens, Baghdad, Cairo, even London, and perhaps one day Washington, DC, we do not find a nation or people "utterly" destroyed.[11] With a nod to the Vatican, no one today would claim Rome or Athens as hubs of empires.

There is another way to interpret this. Walter Brueggemann, as noted by Stulman, has argued that this poem, among other prophetic utterances, was created for worship rather than as a

7. "In chapter 50:2 it says her (Marduk) godlets are disgraced. Gillulim is the word for godlets. It means 'balls of excrement'" (Bright, *Jeremiah*, 353).

8. Lundbom, *Jeremiah 37–52*, 434.

9. Varughese and Modine, *Jeremiah 26–52*, 297.

10. Lundbom, *Jeremiah 37–52*, 368.

11. "Put to the herem" or destroyed in holy war; Bright, *Jeremiah*, 355. There is tension in Scripture itself about the practice of killing everyone and everything. One of the most tragic is described in 1 Sam 3 where King Saul begins his end over this divine policy.

prediction of the future.[12] It is a word of hope that God will do what the repressed people cannot do, namely, take revenge on their enemies. A similar passage can be found in Psalms: "O daughter Babylon, you devastator [or you who are devastated]! Happy shall they be who pay you back what you have done to us! Happy shall they be who take your little ones and dash them against the rock!" (Ps 137:8–9). At the same time, we only need to look at the horrors of Gaza to question the thesis that either Jeremiah or the Psalms are only symbolic. I must ask, in that case, which "God" we are celebrating when making those claims—the Trinity or Mars?

Verse 4 adds, "They shall fall slain in the land of the Chaldeans and wounded in her streets." This verse implies that the young men of the Babylonian army will not die in empire or nation building but in defending their homeland. The arrogance of what had been the greatest nation with the most powerful military ever seen in human history ends on its own streets. Whether it is by the sword of an invading army, a wind that even the strongest cannot resist, or by surrender and murder as prisoners of war, the outcome remains the same. The mighty have fallen.

Verse 5 proclaims why this is so: "Indeed, Israel and Judah have not been forsaken by their God, the LORD of hosts, though their land is full of guilt before the Holy One of Israel." Halfway through this poem, the focus shifts. Brueggemann notes that the word "forsaken" and widowed are related in Hebrew.[13] That the LORD is married to Israel (as both a people and a nation) is an amazing claim and is used in Scripture to describe their relationship for good and ill. In this case, it is for the good. Even combining the separated Israel and Judah, there is a word of hope. For Jeremiah, his focus is on the territory and people of Judah, but Israel is often substituted and implies a complete healing of all twelve tribes as well as the land. The children of Jacob's husband (the LORD) are not dead, although that must have been in question. There is also a reminder of the ongoing theme that God is both God of Israel and Judah as well as LORD of hosts. In other

12. Stulman, *Jeremiah*, 384.

13. Brueggemann, *To Build, to Plant*, 270.

words, there is an intimacy with one particular people alongside sovereignty over all nations. Jeremiah makes this theological claim throughout the book.

This verse immediately following the prediction of the destruction of Babylon raises an important question. Is it possible for God's people to exist as a nation alongside a powerful expansionist empire? In other words, there will be an Israel or there will be a Babylon, but there cannot be both at the same time. These verses seem to point toward a future that is only possible after Babylon has been curtailed, if not destroyed completely. God's people can now be a people in their place and time.

The second half of the verse reminds the reader or listener about why Babylon was needed by God in the first place: the land was full of guilt. Israel/Judah had failed to be the people they were created to be. As noted previously in this thesis, most of that was connected to idolatry or, to stay with the marriage theme, unfaithfulness to her husband. Israel had walked out on the LORD for another husband, who was gold on the outside and dead wood on the inside (Jer 10:3–4).

Verse 6 instructs the reader: "Flee from Babylon; save your lives, each of you! Do not perish because of her guilt, for this is the time of the LORD's vengeance; he is repaying her what is due." It is time for action. This shows a complete shift in Jeremiah's writing. Earlier in the book (37:13 and elsewhere), he is accused of treason because of his advice to surrender to Babylon. Now, he is saying to get out of Babylon. The season has changed. The purpose of Babylon has come to fruition and is about to conclude, and death is not far behind. Brueggemann also suggests that this warning is for other nations who trade or have a shared life with Babylon.[14] It is time to cut the losses, friendships, and head back to your country. The days of prosperous trade and shared livelihood are over. And the end will come quickly.

The theological problem of "the LORD's vengeance" is once again brought into the conversation. John Calvin ties it in with

14. Brueggemann, *Jeremiah*, 270.

theodicy.[15] The "vengeance" against Babylon is tied to justice for Israel/Judah. God's character is at stake here. Will God keep the promise to God's people, or will there be a divorce, or even death? There has been plenty of ink spilt over this part of God's character. There is not a definitive answer. For Jeremiah, the LORD used Babylon as a tool of discipline against God's people who had strayed from the covenant. They had not kept their promise. Once that time of discipline had finished, the purpose of Babylon as an empire was also finished. As noted above, they (both Israel and Babylon, or any other superpower) cannot exist at the same time. God's people will be God's people, and empires will be empires. God's people will continue. Empires come and go. God's justice is revealed in defense of God's people.

"Repaying her [Babylon] what is due" is nothing less than justice for destroying Judah and the temple. Ironically, Babylon was "told" or "allowed" to do it in the first place. Once again, for Jeremiah, the LORD is sovereign over all nations but is married to Israel. Is it possible to chastise without abandonment? Is it possible to chastise to the point where the people believe they have been abandoned? Aside from the Shoah, Jeremiah presents the deepest test of these questions. This verse reclaims both the sovereignty and the fidelity of the LORD.

Verse 7 states, "Babylon was a golden cup in the LORD's hand, making all the earth drunken; the nations drank of her wine, and so the nations went mad." The past tense is important here. As noted above, the purpose of Babylon has come and gone. There is some mystery about the "golden cup." As an empire, certainly there was much wealth poured into the city and nation.[16] There is a certain beauty implied here, and while the hanging gardens of Babylon are not mentioned explicitly, we can assume the reader would be familiar with one of the great wonders of the ancient world. Of course, this makes the statement of destruction even more unlikely, unbelievable, and welcomed, at least by the exiles. There is also uncertainty about what would make all the earth

15. Calvin, *Jeremiah and Lamentations*, 280.

16. Holladay and Hanson, *Jeremiah 2*, 422.

drunk. It could be wealth. It could be violence. The arrogance of Babylon and, secondarily, its allies and trading partners could create a certain "drunkenness" and "madness." Like empire and God's nation's simultaneous existence being incompatible, so is the arrogance of the nations with God's sovereignty. When power, violence, and arrogance combine, a nation has moved away from God's will being done on earth as it is in heaven.

Varughese and Modine sums up this verse:

> Babylon has overstepped the bounds that Yahweh established for it and has therefore called Yahweh's righteous indignation down on its own head. The one who made the whole earth drunk with its violent power will now fall and be broken having itself become drunk on its own power . . . the experience of history is empires always fall; it is just a matter of time.[17]

The "power" created by drunkenness is a delusion. The power created by God choosing to act is not. This brings us back to chapter 25 and the cup that Jeremiah was ordered to have all the nations drink, ending with Babylon and its king (25:26). Here are the continued theological twists found throughout the book. Who is to blame or get credit here? Is it the LORD and Jeremiah in chapter 25, or is it Babylon in 51:7? The outcome is the same. The nations have been affected; the leaders have been affected. Babylon and all those around them are acting like mad, arrogant, insane drunks. This is not finally compatible with God's plan for the world.[18]

Verse 8 reads, "Suddenly Babylon has fallen and is shattered; wail for her! Bring balm for her wound; she may be healed." This is another head-jerking moment in this passage. Is this sarcasm? It is not a surprise that the continued statement of judgment/justice is restated, but why should that be greeted with wailing? One answer is the dread of consequence once the empire falls for both friends and enemies of the empire. All have drunk the golden cup, and the party is over. What will that mean for other peoples and nations' lives and even existence? It is hard to say, but it should be greeted

17. Varughese and Modine, *Jeremiah 26–52*, 296.

18. Miller, "Jeremiah," 917.

with lamentation instead of celebration. Bad water is better than none.

Also implied here is a desire for healing. Again, it is hard to say if this is sarcasm or an honest attempt at reform. We all hope for healing and reform. That hope can lead to desperate measures that may create even more sickness. Finally, this verse reveals the suddenness of the fall. This strong prophetic word is spoken into an empire that seemed invincible. History will show otherwise.

Verse 9 continues with the theme of healing: "We tried to heal Babylon, but she could not be healed. Forsake her and let each of us go to our own country, for her judgment has reached up to heaven and has been lifted even to the skies." Who is the "we" here? Certainly, the exiles have endured the mixed feelings of desiring to return home alongside the enjoyment of a settled life in Babylon. The other nations kept trade and some level of cooperation with the empire that may not have been equal but was certainly mutually beneficial. Here, the attempt at healing recommended in verse 8 has been tried and abandoned. It is too late. There is an uncertain future without Babylon, but that is the future those affected by its influence are heading toward. Will life be better without a Babylon in it? The people are about to find out.

There is a cosmic aspect to this as well: "Her judgment has reached up to heaven and has been lifted up even to the skies" (51:9b). This may mean a couple of different things. First, it may signal that the destruction will be so immense that it will no longer be bound just to the earth. Second, it may be to restate the obvious notion that God has seen the wrong rising all the way to heaven, and God is causing the judgment, or at least allowing it. While this may be a stretch for these texts, historically, it could be said that powerful, violent, arrogant empires do not need divine judgment. They have within their behavior the seeds for their own destruction. For Babylon, the punishment will be extreme.[19] However, if heaven is envisioned as the place and time God's will is done, judgment is fueled by mercy. It is best to have God judge and even punish instead of us.

19. Lundbom, *Jeremiah 37–52*, 442.

Verse 10 concludes the passage: "The LORD has brought forth our vindication; come, let us declare in Zion the work of the LORD our God." This final verse of this pericope comes back to God's people. The time of being punished via Babylon has or will soon end. People expect to return home to Zion. YHWH is mentioned twice in this verse. The first is to declare that the LORD has brought about the vindication, and the second is to declare the LORD's work worthy of praise within God's land—within Zion. The people of Israel, along with other peoples, are preparing to leave the great empire that is doomed. They declare it is time to go home. Let us praise God there.

Jeremiah 51:1–10 serves as a major transition in and a summary of the book of Jeremiah. God will have a people, a nation on earth. Because of their failure to be faithful, they were turned over for seventy years to a foreign land, Babylon. Babylon served its purpose, and because of that loss of purpose, it was destroyed. Unlike Judah, there will be no homecoming for Babylon. Its land has been emptied.

EVERYTHING THAT HAS A BEGINNING ALSO HAS AN END

The book of Jeremiah is a story about God's sovereignty over the nations. Beginning with Israel and extending to all nations, including Babylon. Babylon's existence had a purpose in God's sovereignty, namely, to execute God's judgment on God's people, specifically Judah and Jerusalem, for failing to be the witness to God's will being done on earth as it is in heaven. Babylon also becomes a metaphor in other Scripture, which can be seen most plainly in the books of Daniel and Revelation. It becomes synonymous with empires that have a purpose in God's plan, but only for a certain time. In this essay, I suggest that the same is true for America. From national government to consumerism to climate to division according to class and intolerant political stances, and perhaps the saddest—random massacres of school children. There is little doubt the nation is in a free fall decline. For example, the idol of consumerism is producing one of the greatest wealth disparities in US history. The fruit of that fruit, violence, has led to scapegoating of the poor, particularly immigrants.[20] In March of 2025, we are just beginning to witness the chaos that we have ordered from four years before. We the people wanted more Trump. This time, he is coming with lots of help. It may be America is going to pay for the last five hundred years. Maybe it will land on this generation to settle a debt owed to many peoples and lands. As was said of Babylon, it was right for it to end. It was just. And outside its boundaries, it was celebrated.

The purpose that God may have had for an America is less obvious than its coming demise. It is possible God needed a witness to show the world what human "freedom" will do to humanity, to creation, and possibly to make us hungry for God's kingdom after we see our complete failure at attempting sovereignty. It may be that God has turned us loose to make our own choices and is now allowing us to have the consequences for those choices, that we may turn our hearts toward God as the only hope for life.

This essay will be in conversation with three of the many writers who foresee America's ending. William Stringfellow, Michael Budde, and Chris Hedges offer three different perspectives (theology, political science, and journalism, respectfully) and analyses that eventually point in the same direction: the great experiment of turning humans loose to be free to do as we will is about to end. We have almost destroyed God's creation, as well as each other, in the process.

As someone living within America with hopes and dreams for its (and my) continued prosperity, the notion that the country is doomed scares me. I love my life. Cross-carrying for me today is usually related to trying to work on some bad habit or offering

20. Sherman et al., "Guide to Statistics." From a cynical perspective, could America be defined as a nation that has existed for the accumulation of wealth? Currently, its wealth is concentrated among a few citizens. While McCarraher addresses this more fully, that argument can be traced from Columbus in 1492 to 2025 with the partnership of Donald Trump and Elon Musk. Could much of the Enlightenment language be a veneer for the accumulation of wealth? This is not the whole truth, but it is a long way from the gospel.

forgiveness to a church member full of meddling or muddling habits. That we are near a time of destruction or, to borrow from the dream in the last chapter's excursus, receiving the "order" America has coming fills my heart with angst. Death does not get the final word! But death must come before resurrection.

Throughout Scripture, there is a consistent message that God has created all things seen and unseen, that creation has rebelled in the relationship with God and that God is reconciling creation back to God. For Christians, we are taught that reconciliation comes through Jesus Christ: "For in him all the fullness of God was pleased to reconcile to himself all things whether on earth or in heaven, by making peace through the blood of his cross" (Col 1:19–20). There is hope these days and in this place that, while a possible extinction-level judgment is imminent and obvious, it is a means to an end, and that, as Matt 3:12 suggests, the wheat will be gathered into the barn. Can we dare celebrate the burning of the chaff?

Three years ago, I met with a surgeon regarding a clavicle I had broken in a motorcycle accident. The bone was broken in four places and would require a metal plate to be whole again. It was not going to repair itself, nor was it an injury I could heal on my own. However, the surgeon was not going to repair my entire body, just the broken part. Is it possible we could see God's judgment in this way? We need a surgeon (or a Great Physician). The good news is that while the healing was painful and expensive, it has led to restoration.

William Stringfellow, in two of his works, *An Ethic for Christians and Other Aliens in a Strange Land*[21] and *Conscience and Obedience: The Politics of Romans 13 and Revelation 13 in Light of the Second Coming*,[22] extends the need for judgment/surgery beyond individuals to the principalities and powers. Extending a doctrine of the fall from Gen 3, he looks at organizations, including nations and corporations, as also needing the wheat separated from the chaff. In the time and place he wrote; he witnessed a lot

21. Stringfellow, *Ethic for Christians*.

22. Stringfellow, *Conscience and Obedience*.

of chaff! Vietnam, the beginnings of neoliberal economics, and a growing skepticism of truthfulness from the leadership in Washington, DC, gave plenty of fuel for Stringfellow's argument. It is tame compared to today. The veneer of a nation for the people by the people has been torn off and those who own and control this country are now out in the open and apparently ruling as they will.

"All have sinned and fall short of the glory of God" (Rom 3:23). Likewise, in the days of Jeremiah, all the nations, especially Babylon, had reached the same place (see especially chapters 46–51). Their usefulness to God's plan to reconcile creation had ended. Only a remnant of Judah would remain. For Stringfellow, "Babylon is the parable of the nation beheld in the manifold dimensions of the nation's actual, fallen existence in history."[23] Christians understand the fallenness of the individual; Stringfellow argues this is also true of all of creation, all the nations, including America.[24]

Stringfellow organizes the judgment around that which leads to death and that which leads to life. For him, death is the very power behind the powers.[25] Life is wheat; death is chaff. Jeremiah testifies to the winnowing necessary to separate wheat from chaff, but this work will require Jesus. To help with understanding this, Stringfellow sets up a dichotomy between Jerusalem and Babylon. Jerusalem represents God's redemption of creation, or the wheat, and Babylon, the chaff.[26] With echoes of Cavanaugh's warnings of idolatry, Babylon lives in a delusion that it is either already Stringfellow's understanding of Jerusalem or will be.[27] Babylon has become an idol. Much of this can be found in America's claim to be the new Jerusalem as well as the claim that it is the "greatest nation in history."

> Babylon's futility is her idolatry—her boast of justifying significance or moral ultimacy in her destiny, her

23. Stringfellow, *Ethic for Christians*, 50.

24. Stringfellow, *Ethic for Christians*, 27, and throughout much of the book.

25. Bill Wylie-Kellerman, "Foreword to 2004 Edition," in Stringfellow, *Ethic for Christians.*

26. Stringfellow, *Ethic for Christians*, 48.

27. Cavanaugh, *Uses of Idolatry*.

> reputation, her capabilities, her authority, her glory as a nation. The moral pretenses of Imperial Rome, the millennial claims of Nazism, the arrogance of Marxist dogma, the anxious insistence that America be "number one" among nations are all versions of Babylon's idolatry. All share in this grandiose view of the nation by which the principality assumes the place of God in the world.[28]

The good news in all that is that America is not alone. The shocking news is that all those empires were judged, and at least in Rev 18:20, that demise is celebrated. As covered in this chapter's exegesis, Jeremiah reveals that God can continue to work with the nations, including the Babylons, despite the idolatry. They can still be useful for God's purposes for a while. When those purposes are fulfilled, however, the chaff is burned. The nations exist to serve God, who desires peace on earth good will to all; God does not exist to serve the nations.

This argument creates several theological problems regarding the sovereignty of God. We see an explicit story of this in Gen 18:16–33, where an incredible debate occurs between Abraham and God regarding God's sovereignty over Sodom. It is not a fair debate! But God indulges in it. There seems to be some agency given to humans inside God's rule. This gets more complicated when we have the stories of Joshua, Babylon in Jer 51, the destruction of Jerusalem in 70 CE, and of course, the Shoah. Claiming God's sovereignty in horror stands in tension if not complete contradiction with the God who reveals merciful love. Even if the just and unjust are swept up together in death, the Great Winnower has the final word. How God can be love and judge and sovereign and almighty is beyond comprehension. My only appeal at this point is to 1 Cor 15:19, "If for this life only we have hoped in Christ, we are of all people most to be pitied." Eventually, there will be death. And eventually, in Christ Jesus, there will be life.

Until then, the struggle between the two continues. Stringfellow notices the irony of how Christians are taught to see the Bible as a non-political book, but America uses the Bible as a means of

28. Stringfellow, *Ethic for Christians*, 51.

justifying its politics.[29] Throughout Scripture, creation is ordered by the sovereignty of God. It is disordered by sin and death that comes with it. As noted in Willie Jennings's work, colonialism and the genocide and chattel slavery that came with it were all justified using Scripture.[30] The Bible was (is!) used to justify public policy. However, at least in much popular preaching, the Bible is discussed primarily as a road map to lead individual souls away from hell and into heaven.[31] Nations, corporations, even churches are oddly left out. Stringfellow helps us see this is a serious omission:

> As a social ethic, this concentration upon the efficacious potential of individuals, even when computed geometrically, suffers the distortion of any partial truth. That is, what it overlooks or omits is more significant than that which it asserts and affirms. What is most crucial about this situation, biblically speaking, is the failure of moral theology, in the American context, to confront the principalities—the institutions, systems, ideologies, and other political and social powers—as militant, aggressive, and immensely influential creatures in this world as it is.[32]

Jeremiah 46–51 demonstrates that the nations are judged just as much as individuals. Part of that judgment, as was discussed concerning idolatry, is how the nations claim sovereignty over God. Or more malevolently, claim to be "under God" while serving death. Delusion is hard to identify, much less repent from, by those caught in it.

Fortunately, we have Scripture to help lead us to the truth. In Gen 3:5, the serpent's lie that we can be like God applies to much more than just humans. Michael Budde gives a fifty-year update on Stringfellow's perspective:

29. Stringfellow, *Ethic for Christians*, 15.

30. Jennings, *Christian Imagination*.

31. "Evangelical" preaching, modernized by Billy Graham and others, emphasizes atonement almost to the exclusion of the gospel themes of justice and mercy. Popular preaching that is basically group psychological therapy is beyond the subject of this work.

32. Stringfellow, *Ethic for Christians*, 17.

> Modern citizenship and modern nation states are not "natural." They are products of power plays and indoctrination, slaughter and conquest, coincidence, and coercion. To equate citizenship with a natural reality that Christians are obliged to love is a mistake of historic importance.[33]

As a pastor in America for over thirty years, the thought that Christians are not to love America as we love Jesus is almost beyond speech. Stringfellow and Budde claim we have been taught to love chaff.

This goes well beyond sentiment. The economic system in America has "made the nations drunk" (Jer 51:7) and is unsustainable: "unlimited economic expansion, which is a constitutive feature of capitalism, and the political regimes associated with it, is impossible in a bounded and limited biosphere."[34] We live and are taught to love the "American way of life" that is killing itself. It is consuming itself. Even the meager attempts at sustainability and something that looks like the kingdom of God, inclusive of "all," have been rolled back by capitalism's finest. The shifting political sands that are held in sway of an economic system that exists only to make money. This system moves from pride flags to Trump flags, depending on the bottom line.

While the climate catastrophe is beyond the parameters of this project, it is vital to much scientific and theological work today. For our purposes, Budde underlines the inevitable outcome of an economic system (that McCarraher and Cavanaugh identify as idolatrous) that is destroying God's creation.[35] How can such a system be allowed to continue? How can a nation that cannot exist outside of that system continue? Who is sovereign?

Another piece of death chaff is violence. Depending on how "war" is defined, some estimate America has been at war for 93 percent of its history.[36] Scripture reveals a God who has defeated

33. Budde, *Foolishness to Gentiles*, 18.

34. Budde, *Foolishness to Gentiles*, 34.

35. McCarraher, *Enchantments of Mammon*; Cavanaugh, *Uses of Idolatry.*

36. Oord, "Believe It or Not."

death and is bringing eternal life into God's creation. The kingdom of God and America are heading in opposite directions. Again, Stringfellow notes,

> All virtues which nations elevate and idolize—military prowess, material abundance, technological sophistication, imperial grandeur, high culture, racial pride, trade, prosperity, conquest, sport, language, or whatsoever—are ancillary and subservient to the moral presence of death in the nation.[37]

While America is not alone is this testimony to that which Jesus has defeated, it is certainly not outside the realm of God's sovereignty and may be leading the pack as the current Babylon. Certainly, Stringfellow thinks so. Much of my work as a pastor and in this thesis is attempting to create some space between Christian discipleship and the violence assumed to necessarily accompany it. It is no easy task, as violence seems to be the water in which American Christians swim.

Violence is not the only factor incompatible with God's plan for God's world. Lying will also die (Rev 21:5). Budde argues,

> For the American experiment, like all imperial projects, has been built on lies . . . these lies made America possible and the Church has helped fashion these lies . . . strategic forgetting, whitewashing and projection allowed for the American story to be one of a chosen people, the pinnacle of social evolution—the lie that is known as American exceptionalism.[38]

If war and lies are chaff, much of what America is stands in the same judgment as Babylon. Now that the modern Nebuchadnezzar has retaken the throne, we can count on additions to the *Washington Post*'s tally of lies Donald Trump made during his first term as president, which numbered over thirty thousand.[39]

37. Stringfellow, *Ethic for Christians*, 68.

38. Budde, *Foolishness to Gentiles*, 38.

39. Kessler et al., "Trump's False or Misleading Claims."

I realize the imminent demise of America is not a hard argument to make. Budde states the obvious: making the case that the American empire is in irreversible decline is an easier matter [than the ambiguous goals of settler colonialism discussed just prior in his essay], at least in terms of finding support for the trend across a variety of disciplines and ideological dispositions.[40] The ambiguity is introduced when analysis shifts from the principality and power to individual Americans. As a pastor for over thirty years, I can attest that all the Christians with whom I have interacted seem capable of practicing both Christianity and American citizenship, even patriotism. Both the cross and soldiers are grafted together as being "under God." Individual violent and dishonest actors are often written off as exceptions, even though, as I write this, there are two soldiers, one decorated, accused of terrorist acts on New Year's Eve 2025.[41] Budde and Stringfellow argue these acts are symptoms of a much deeper fallenness.

As the world is heading toward a time when wars shall cease (Isa 2:4), America's final global influence is in war making:

> With its economic power diminished and its comparative advantage eroding steadily, the United States no longer has nearly unmatched influence in any area of world political economy—not in production, not in finance, nor in innovation, nor in rulemaking. Where it remains unmatched to date is around military force.[42]

It becomes a stretch when the only answer for why America needs over 750 military bases overseas is "to defend freedom." Even that is incompatible with the gospel. The work of a Christian is to daily surrender our "freedom" over to Jesus to use as he will. The Christian life is dedicated to daily cross carrying, not doing whatever we want (Luke 9:23 and Rom 12:2).

With regards to making the entire world drunk, as Babylon is accused of, Budde warns the Catholic Church in Africa not

40. Budde, *Foolishness to Gentiles*, 44.

41. See Gentry, "Very Strange Similarities," among many other various news websites.

42. Budde, *Foolishness to Gentiles*, 46.

to follow the empire off the cliff. While his lecture is limited to African Catholics, I am sure the same could be said for American Protestants, perhaps even more so. Of many warnings, some covered above, here he connects the church, America, and race, acknowledging that the gospel always enculturates. In America, however, it was enculturated into the wrong things:

> It is important to understand that the American identity on offer to Catholics in the nineteenth and twentieth centuries was very much a racialized one with a political economy and cultural ecology built upon stratifications and classifications that structured outcomes such that lower groups were exploited or excluded so that the upper groups could enjoy long term and self-sustaining advantages.[43]

While Jennings spends much of his work on this topic, it is obvious today this racial stratum is still in place.[44] So once again, it must be asked, empowered by visions of the new heaven and new earth like that found in Rev 7:9, where peoples from every nation, tribe, and language gather together, how can American racial hierarchies and all that come with those contribute to God's plan for the world?

Turning to Chris Hedges, in his 2018 book *America: The Farewell Tour*, he uses his journalism skills to add testimonies to Stringfellow's and Budde's analyses. Hedges provides interviews of individuals from across America and offers analysis regarding the opiate crisis, pornography, racism, and the financial devastation that is encouraged by various sorts of legal gambling.[45] America is coming apart.

With regards to racialized hate, little debate about the observation made by Dr. Martin Luther King Jr., who may have borrowed this line from Malcom X, that Sunday morning is very segregated. Racial fear and hatred are "niced" up more now but can easily be witnessed in the church. The newer declines covered by Hedges

43. Budde, *Foolishness to Gentiles*, 84.

44. Jennings, *Christian Imagination*.

45. Hedges, *America*.

are very much affecting the people I pastor and community as well. The opioid crisis (the roots of which are exposed in Patrick Keefe's *Empire of Pain: The Secret History of the Sackler Dynasty*) continues to wreak havoc in our community.[46] Deaths from overdoses on Fentanyl compete with methamphetamine addiction. I conducted a funeral for a young man recently who died from an encounter with one or the other or both. The church was full of his young grieving friends, including his drug dealer. In Hedges's chapter on pornography, I suffered through over ten pages of some of the most horrific stories I have ever read of torture—all justified under the banner of "sexual freedom." It is almost entirely sexual exploitation of women, many of whom are trying to feed the very drug habits mentioned above. It is with great irony that I have just as many United Methodist church members (and perhaps some colleagues) who have gambling as a hobby, mostly the lottery, that I am aware of, an activity that is explicitly forbidden in our Book of Discipline. That I have been engaged in debates about the "incompatibility with Scripture" regarding homosexuality for thirty-plus years only to see the same people shrug shoulders at the rules against gambling further fuels much of what this essay is trying to expose. We continue to strain out gnats and swallow camels (Matt 23:24).

In his last chapter, "Freedom," Hedges takes aim at the final virtue of America: democracy. He writes,

> These liberal institutions . . . collapsed under sustained assault during the past forty years of corporate power. They exist only in name. They are props for the democratic facade. Liberal non-profits, from MoveOn.org to the Sierra Club, are no better. They are feeble appendages to a corporatized Democratic Party. There are . . . no institutions left in America that can authentically be called democratic.[47]

Hedges holds little, if any, hope for a solution.

46. Keefe, *Empire of Pain*.

47. Hedges, *America*, 249.

It is possible, even likely, that the great experiment of majority rule, and perhaps, more importantly, a belief that the decisions of the majority reveal the truth, is ending. It is leading away from an ethic of "love your neighbor as yourself." It is leading away from peace on earth, good will to all. If America was ever in harmony with the kingdom of God, it is certainly out of tune now. Violence, greed, deification of the nation and white people, deification of capitalism and "progress" have brought us to this point. The idol is proving to be worthless. Where and to whom shall we go? Is there not some good news?

SERMON

The intended audience for this sermon presents a bit of a conundrum. It could easily be adapted for a gathering of the Ekklesia Project, where it would be met with a few polite nods, but there would be nothing new for them here. It could be preached at my current appointment in Caldwell County, North Carolina, where 87 percent of voters helped reelect Donald Trump president of the United States. They may agree with much of the critique of the current state of America but would add that Mr. Trump is Jesus' appointed savior for America. The thought that God's use for America may be nearing its end seems incompressible to the place and time where I work and live. If what is written below is the word of God for the people of God, it will, to one group or another, be preached. Jeremiah was not allowed to remain silent.

The End Is Near: A Sermon on Jeremiah 51:1–10

God and Jeremiah have been on world tour. In chapters 46 through 51 of the book of Jeremiah, all the nations of the known world are coming under God's judgment. They have failed to be useful to God's plan for God's world. Today, in chapter 51, we get to the final, lone superpower, Babylon. Our lesson begins with the awe-inspiring phrase, "Thus says the LORD." As we know, when we see that name in all caps, it is code for YHWH, the name spoken to Moses at the burning bush some eight hundred years before. *I AM WHO I AM. I WILL BE WHO I AM.*

Much of these chapters on the nations, including but not limited to Israel and Judah, has to do with God's sovereignty. That is not a word or an idea we use much today, and there may be some reasons for that. Some of the ways Merriam-Webster defines "sovereignty" is as "supreme power especially over a body politic" and "freedom from external control." Though the definition of "sovereignty" can and will expand a bit, in this, we find the source of the conflict of our passage today. Who is sovereign? Is it a group of people or a nation exercising its self-proclaimed "supreme power" to be self-governing and "free from external control," or is it I AM? The entire book of Jeremiah, and most explicitly in the passage we are focusing on today, says I AM is sovereign. I AM governs. I AM has supreme authority.

Babylon, among others, challenges that. They had a lot of worldly power. From the world's greatest military to the hanging gardens of Nebuchadnezzar, Babylon had it all. It was, at the time, the greatest nation ever. They had even been given power over God's chosen people, over what was left of Israel.

Our passage today challenges their claims to sovereignty. It begins, "Thus says the LORD: I am going to stir up a destructive wind against Babylon and against the inhabitants of Leb-qamai or Chaldea" (51:1). Babylon is about to encounter a force outside of itself—outside of its "rights"—outside of its claimed sovereignty. The greatest nation in history is about to find out who is Lord of the nations.

But as soon as this pronouncement is made, we have a subtle question. Verse 2 reads, "And I will send winnowers to Babylon, and they shall winnow her." I imagine it has been a while since any of us have done any winnowing—the tossing of wheat into the air with the heavier kernels falling to the floor and the lighter chaff flying off. What is needed is a gentle but firm breeze, not a destructive wind that will take the wheat with the chaff. We will take a closer look at what sort of sovereign I AM is in the final sermon in this series, but for today, we know the judgment can be, and hopefully will be, more subtle than carpet bombing or "shock and awe."

However, Jeremiah is not going to let anyone breathe easily. Even though the winnowers work with a gentle, non-destructive wind, the effect will be to "empty her land when they come against her from every side on the day of trouble" (v. 2). Destructive or not, the wind is going to create something different. It will remove Babylon's claim to sovereignty. It will remove Babylon's claim as the greatest nation ever. It will come fast, and it will be complete.

Verses 3 and 4 have a couple of different images that lead to the same end. "Let not the archer bend his bow and let him not array himself in his coat of mail." Is this directed at the winnowers or the soldiers of Babylon who are to defend the nation? If directed at the winnowers, it may mean there is no need to fight or protect; God has this. If it is directed at the Babylonian military, it may be understood as there being no need to defend the nation. It is futile to fight back. Either way, I AM is claiming power.

But how that power is claimed is a mystery. We know from history that when Cyrus of Persia became the next greatest leader of the next greatest nation ever, it was almost nonviolent. Babylon collapsed without a lot of struggles. Perhaps the command to "not spare her young men; utterly destroy her entire army" may mean the soldiers simply walked off the job. There was not anything left worth defending.

I want to dare into a comparison that will probably anger, if not enrage, some of you. But it is a true story. I met a retired US Army soldier. He had served this country in the military for over twenty years. He had served in Iraq. Had guarded Saddam Hussein's sons. He also, in his words, "guarded the desert." During that time, he had a revelation. He asked himself, "What am I doing here? What are we doing here?" He then assessed his entire career: "The only thing we ever did for this country was during Hurricane Katrina. We got in there and worked hard and really helped the American people. Everything else we have done has been a waste of time and money."

I realize this is only one testimony, although it is an important one. But what if some of the Babylonian soldiers felt the same way? They had taken over the entire known world, and for what? Their country was falling apart at home. Why even pull a bow or put on armor? Just let it go.

Again, if you will indulge me for speaking out of my mind: Is it possible, if not probable, that this country idolizes the military? That the United States military is lifted as a kind of sovereign? That it is seen as a god-like institution that blinds it and us to the truth?

Part of that problem, according to either Budde or Stringfellow, is how soldiers who have sacrificed their lives for the nation are remembered. Is there a way to do that truthfully without turning the military into an idol that will be subject to a destructive wind or winnowing or both?

I was pastor of a man named Harry Burnette at Long's United Methodist Church in Canton, North Carolina. Harry was in worship every Sunday. He went to Sunday School. He was in charge of the biscuits on men's breakfast Sunday. Harry was also a veteran. But well beyond that, he was a POW in World War II and was tortured by the Japanese. I have heard that his torture was as we could imagine. When he came home, Harry was never the same. In his service to this country, he sacrificed who he was and wanted to be. Much of that died in Japan. Harry was considered a hero. No questions asked.

At the same time, similarly to my Iraq vet friend, another soldier once shared on Veteran's Day: "Don't thank me for my service. My whole time in the military was spent getting drunk and having sex with prostitutes."

There is a god-like status that is given to soldiers and the military that calls Christians to consider some significant questions, if not complete repentance. How can we say thank you to Harry without flirting with sovereignty? Is there a way to evaluate military service, even service in combat, with truthfulness that does not tip over into idolatry? More importantly, if the devil is speaking the truth in Luke 4:6 that all authority of the nations has been given over to him/them, soldiers and those who support war must honestly ask whom is being served in this conflict?[48] Is it the devil?

Eventually, the One true God is revealed, and there is no other. To be fair, individuals in America enter military service today for many reasons. To label any of them as imperialists or even patriotic might be a stretch. Perhaps God has even called some. Jesus' encounter with the Roman centurion in Luke 7 not only resulted in a miraculous healing but the faith of the commander being called out as exemplary. At the same time, the devil's claim just three chapters before of having authority over the kingdoms of the world must be discerned with care and help from the Holy Spirit. God gets the final word over the nations.

Part of that we can see hinted at in verse 5: "Indeed, Israel and Judah have not been forsaken by their God, the LORD of hosts, though their land is full of guilt before the Holy One of Israel."

This inevitably leads to another complex issue. The relationship between the church and Israel is complicated, beautiful, and tragic. The church, both Protestant and Catholic, has made claims to sovereignty as well. For today, I hope Paul's metaphor will be adequate: gentile Christians are a "wild olive shoot grafted onto the cultivated tree" (Rom 11:24). We share in God's promises to Israel—or better said, in today's world, the children of Jacob—as friends. We share in the promise to Abraham that God will bless all nations. So, to the list of those in verse 5 who have not been forsaken by God despite their guilt, with a great deal of humility, we add the church; we add those of us who believe the Messiah has come. Much discussion could be added to the segment of the church that embraces dispensational theology and the Christian Zionism that comes with. Anything that involves killing, whether Jew or Palestinian, must be seriously questioned as to being guided by the Holy Spirit or the Prince of Peace. Much of Christian Zionism

48. This opens up an eschatological question of who has the authority post-ascension. Perhaps, living as the kingdom of God is both here and yet to come is a good starting place. The authority of the devil is defeated but still being exercised in many places, including the nations. The ending danger is even worse as the time is short (Rev 12:12).

is a witness to the triumphalism and, especially, the violence that stands before the Judge of the nations.

Getting back to our passage, even if America joins Babylon in the winnowing, the followers of Jesus and the children of Jacob need not despair. Israel has seen its country destroyed more than once. America was torn apart during the Civil War, and there are many signs that something worse may be blowing. The people of God, Jew and gentile, have survived. That survival in our present day may depend on knowing that we have not been forsaken as we also follow the urgent advice from verse 6 to "flee from the midst of Babylon; save your lives, each of you!"

Here again, I want to offer a literal and metaphorical interpretation of this verse. Some have left America. Some will leave. Some have no choice.

But a more faithful, cross-carrying life is the arduous work of staying within America, the modern Babylon, if we will, and living here in a right and faithful relationship with the nation. America is either losing or has already lost its sovereignty in the world. About all it has left is the power of the military, and as has been noted above, we would do well not to engage in idolizing that. The church could find a way to follow Jesus inside America. If this is the calling of the Holy Spirit, then so be it. If so, we would do well to study closely the work of people like Stanley Hauerwas, who has spent his career encouraging the church to be a witness of peace; William Stringfellow, who has unveiled the sin of the principalities and powers, including the nations; and Mike Budde, who brings the skill of a Christian political scientist. All three of these authors offer a truthful critique of America alongside a truthful call to follow Jesus as Lord. The truth is being spoken by some. Will we have ears to hear? Can we hear a voice of peace that passes all understanding? A peace that comes not from violence or threat of violence but from the cross and resurrection?

One immediate thing that needs to stop is the desperate chasing of whatever false messiah comes along with a simple solution. I cannot go as far as to suggest today that Christians should give up on reforming America. But Jeremiah tells us that, at least regarding

Babylon, it is useless: "Bring balm for her wound; perhaps she may be healed. We tried to heal Babylon, but she could not be healed" (51:8b–9a).

For us, it is about what we do. If there is a strong parallel between Babylon and America, or any other superpower before or after, if we are trying to have ultimate faith in some sort of comeback or reform that could result from electing new leaders, it may be hopeless. We really need to hear and accept that. History shows us that some nations rise in power and authority and all of them eventually fail. To think that America is immune to this is delusional.

However, Christians could repent of our idolatry of America, and the military, and anything else we look to be sovereign in this world besides the lordship of Jesus Christ. We must seek first the kingdom of God. When our worship, our hearts, our allegiances are given completely to that, we can have much hope. Our witness can be faithful no matter what else happens.

We cannot control what I AM may or may not do with America. But we can control, with a great deal of hope, how well we live into the lordship of Jesus Christ and his sovereignty. He is Lord of all nations, including America.

Revelation 22:2 describes the river of life coming out of the new Jerusalem with the tree of life providing fruit for the healing of the nations. Our hope is that America is included in that healing. Repentance from violence and greed will be needed. Repentance from destroying what God has created will be needed. There is some doubt about what will be left. But there are witnesses. There are those; I worship with them every Sunday and I am sure anyone reading these words does as well, who live close to Matt 25:31–46 and live life in service to the least of these. Many of them carry the cross in one hand and the American flag in the other.

We may be in for some cross-carrying days. Particularly, those who expect more from this country than it can provide. More than reform may be necessary. A new heart may be necessary. Ask any who have lost their homes or declared bankruptcy over medical or school debt, those who are lost in addiction themselves or are witness to a friend's addiction, and they will tell you about the cross. Ask those who can see we are using up God's gift of creation and throwing it away. It seems to be in spirit as a people to use up and throw away—often, as quickly as possible. But, as with any generalization, there is a contradictory witness. There is hope in the heart of the people and perhaps in the heart of the nation.

Verse 10 ends in a word of hope: "The LORD has brought forth our vindication; come let us declare in Zion the work of the LORD our God." What exactly that may mean for Christians living within the boundaries of America is uncertain. But we could serve the LORD who is still at work—who is still bringing a new heaven and a new earth, who is still bringing both justice and peace to *all* the world. May we rededicate ourselves to following this God today. To following Jesus today. There will be no stopping God's justice, whatever that may look like. But we know that after the cross comes a resurrection. Amen.

CONCLUSION

Language is inadequate to describe what is about to happen. Jeremiah helps us to speak into that which cannot be spoken. There is no longer any blame. There is no longer any rational explanation. That which seemed to be eternal is found to be temporary. That which seemed to be refined gold is found to be a cover for a wooden idol with clay feet. It cannot save, and if Jeremiah is speaking a word of truth today, neither will it be saved.

God continues to speak. That word will continue until all things are reconciled. We just do not know how much we will have to sacrifice in the process. Hope has the final word. Jesus Christ and his kingdom, complete with a new heaven and a new earth, has the final word. History is proving that hope in America is misplaced. Jesus will decide how much, if any, of America will be healed and allowed to participate in his kingdom. Of many places in Scripture, including Jeremiah's book of consolation, explored in the next chapter are Jesus' departing words in Matthew: "All authority in heaven and on earth has been given to me. . . . I am with you always, to the end of the age" (28:18, 20). It is a true hope—a hope that cannot be overcome or altered. In the concluding chapter, we will embrace that hope. May it sustain us when all else is lost.

CHAPTER 4

HOPE

God will not abandon that which God creates. Both Old Testament and New include hardship and death, but there is always a final word: life. I follow that lead. It may be that America and the church within it will suffer to the extreme that Judah and the people suffered. We will see. However, suffering and death are never the last word. The God of love, light, and hope gets the final word. Hauerwas and Willimon, in their book *The Holy Spirit*, give a revelation of hope: "*The fellowship in the Spirit makes Christians love one another and, in particular, love one another for how our differences are crucial for the upbuilding of the body of Christ.*"[1] There is a need for a shift: more faith in Jesus and the continued and ultimate triumph of his kingdom and less, if any at all, in the empire known as America.

Almost in the center of this amazing book, Jeremiah is told by the LORD to speak a word of hope—a word of consolation to those who either have or are about to lose everything. Chapters 30 to 33 are known as "the book of consolation.[2] Below is an exegesis, essay, and sermon on vital portion of this section, 31:23–40.

1. Hauerwas and Willimon, *Holy Spirit*, 57. Italics theirs.

2. Fretheim, *Jeremiah*, 413. Of the commentators I reviewed, there is consensus for using this description for these chapters.

EXEGESIS OF JEREMIAH 31:23–40

Verse 23 begins, "Thus says the LORD of hosts, the God of Israel: Once more they shall use these words in the land of Judah and in its town when I restore their fortunes: The LORD bless you, O abode of righteousness, O holy hill!" In this complex book, we must always pause when we read, "Thus saith the LORD." This phrase here introduces a promise of restoration and consolation from the One first introduced to Moses at the burning bush. I AM's word causes the change it declares. While Judah and Israel seem interchangeable in Jeremiah, here it is implied that together, they form a restored nation. All of Jacob's children's land and people are together as one. Jeremiah then moves from the whole to the book's main topic: Judah, home to David's city and Solomon's temple. At that time these words were written, most likely, both had been destroyed. Judah and Jerusalem had become curse words. However, when this new word is fulfilled, they will become part of a blessing.

Assuming the "abode of righteousness" is Jerusalem and the temple, this also implies a healing of its loss. When Nebuchadnezzar was given power over it, it was far from righteous. These words, which help create reality, speak of a time when "I will be their God, and they will be my people" (31:33). Lundbom confirms that "O holy mountain" is an honorific title for Jerusalem. Lundbom goes on to note that this blessing cannot be spoken with Jerusalem and the temple in ruins, but it will be said once again.[3] Brueggemann, commenting on verses 23–25 says, "This promissory oracle again anticipates resumed renewed life in the land. The poem asserts God's resolve to invert completely every aspect of Judah's life."[4] Fretheim suggests this is a personal word from God to God's suffering people and believes that, since it refers to land, it is connected to Abraham.[5] Bracke comments on verses 23–30,

3. Lundbom, *Jeremiah 21–36*, 456.

4. Brueggemann, *Jeremiah*, 288.

5. Fretheim, *Jeremiah*, 413–14.

"Grumbling about the fairness of God's judgment will cease and the appropriateness of God's justice will be recognized.[6]

Supersessionism has been (and can continue to be) a highly consequential sin the church has committed against the Jews. The belief of the church that Christians have replaced the Jews as God's people are found within the writings of John Calvin. Discussing verse 24, he argues, "He speaks here about the restoration of the church. That its restored state will be in no way inferior to its previous state. Its inhabitants in the villages and country places will not be less secure than those in the cities."[7] That this theology is passed along to the Puritans no doubt helped gave birth to the idolatrous worship and creation of America as the "new Jerusalem."

Verse 24 continues, "And Judah and all its towns shall live there together, and the farmer and those who wander with their flocks." This suggests that the restoration will be both an infrastructure rebuild and a repopulation. Reconciliation is an important theme in chapters 30 through 33. Here, it is between the farmers and the shepherds—historical rivals going all the way back to Cain and Abel in Gen 4:1–16.[8]

Verse 25 adds a pastoral promise: "I will satisfy the weary, and all who are faint I will replenish." Lundbom identifies this passage's language as "prophetic perfects," which means it refers to such a solid promise that it is like it has already happened.[9]

Verse 26 makes a turn that is the subject of significant difference of opinion. It reads, "Thereupon I awoke and looked, and my sleep was pleasant to me." There are hypotheses regarding who "awoke" that range from Jeremiah to even God. As someone who has woken from a few of these divinely inspired dreams, I would not use the word "pleasant," but certainly "in awe" would be appropriate.[10] Regardless of who may be waking here, this is a verse of hope.

6. Bracke, *Jeremiah 30–52*, 21.
7. Calvin, *Jeremiah and Lamentations*, 187.
8. Lundbom, *Jeremiah 21–36*, 457.
9. Lundbom, *Jeremiah 21–36*, 457.
10. See the excursus at the end of chapter 2.

Verse 27 appears to continue the theme of verse 25, but this time with a promise beyond the pastoral: "The days are surely coming, says the LORD, when I will sow the house of Israel and the house of Judah with the seed of humans and the seed of animals." This is the Great Sower who not only promises to recreate both people and animals (and provide all that they need to prosper), but also to reconcile the northern and southern kingdoms. This is an amazing, beyond-human work promise. The verb translated here as "I will" (found in this verse and throughout this passage), according to Stulman, is so strong that "it almost eliminates the openness of God to human choices."[11] It is not up to the returning exiles nor to the principalities and powers found in Babylon. YHWH is making this happen. Berrigan says that for anything "new" to emerge, a newness that will spell a veritable rebirth of spirit, "Yahweh must venture a prodigious first step."[12] That is a good summary of the entire "book of consolation."

Verse 28 deserves its own thesis. It reads, "And just as I have watched over them to pluck up and break down, to overthrow, destroy, and bring evil, so I will watch over them to build and to plant, says the LORD." What sort of God is YHWH that can both destroy and restore? What sort of people can lose everything, including the city and temple they thought had been promised *by this God* to never be lost, and still have faith this word can come true? What sort of relationship is necessary for this to happen?

However fragile it may have been, it was enough. Ezra and Nehemiah give us the testimony that this indeed happened. Well beyond the power of the exiles, the exile begins to end. Cyrus of Persia defeated Babylon and, in one executive order, allowed the exiles to go home. To hear "I will watch over them to build and to plant" in the midst of the rubble requires an almost blind faith. Jeremiah reveals a God who is sovereign over all peoples and nations. Inside that sovereignty are cloaked characteristics of mercy and justice. As implied in verse 27, here there is a mixed metaphor, "to build and to plant." The vision is rural and urban, concerning

11. Stulman, *Jeremiah*, 271.

12. Berrigan, *Jeremiah*, 132.

farming and construction. Both activities require human participation, and both require strength from God. God and humans create, destroy, and, in this case, restore.

Brueggemann comments,

> Verse 28 appeals to the six verbs which set the theme of the Jeremiah tradition in 1:10. The four negative verbs are intensified by the addition of a fifth one, "to bring evil." The most important matter in this verse is that the five negative verbs have all been fully enacted. There is no more threat in them.[13]

Still, the notion of a God who "brings evil" is one I find problematic. All of the commentators I reviewed carefully avoided this question. If the English is translated "judgment" instead of "evil," then it makes a sort of sense. Judgment can be a means to grace and forgiveness—to build and to plant once again. The theological problem could be softened by translating the word as "disaster."[14] However, questions of theodicy arise in Jeremiah. Rejecting evil as an end in itself, translating God's activity as "bringing disaster" leaves open the possibility that this devastating divine activity is a last resort; a necessary means.

Verse 29 moves on to consider an old proverb: "In those days they shall no longer say: 'The parents have eaten sour grapes, and the children's teeth are set on edge.'" This proverb was quoted widely following the exile.[15] Time is important in this passage. While it is mostly about the future, it evokes the past, which the proverb makes explicit. For a modern interpreter with some knowledge of family systems, this proverb is especially interesting. Intentionally or not, "sin" or "disorder" tends to run in families, communities, and nations. One explanation for this "inheritance" is that God causes the sin to be passed along in some sort of "original" package. This verse implies that at the least the consequences of the sins of the previous generation will no longer fall on the present

13. Brueggemann, *Jeremiah*, 290.

14. REB.

15. Lundbom, *Jeremiah 21–36*, 461.

generation. There is not enough here to refute the doctrine of original sin; however, there is a promise of some sort of new future not trapped by the past. Once again, it is something the LORD will need to make happen.

There is also a practical consequence that I hope will prove true today. My parents' generation and my own have not given much care to creation. We have all but destroyed it. My children, their generation, and those who follow will most likely have their "teeth set on edge" due to our carelessness. May the promise of this verse, that there will be days in the future when the next generation will not suffer the consequences of our past actions, come true! God is going to have to make this happen. Otherwise, the edgy teeth will continue to be passed along.

In verse 30, the old Jeremiah returns! "But all shall die for their own sins; the teeth of everyone who eats sour grapes shall be set on edge." We are not looking at a utopia here, but there is still healing. There is a restoration of what might be pure free will. For example, an adult child might behave in line with or in rebellion against a parent. In some, perhaps unconscious way, the will is determined by a parent. The sin is inherited. The behavior of one is influenced (if not decided) by another. This verse says sins will still happen and still have consequences, but the propensity for sin will be healed. That there would still be sin at all and why is a great question. How might a human be free to choose not to sin? This verse points us toward a future promise where God will do for us what we cannot do for ourselves. For example, I would hope anyone reading this book, including myself, would not intentionally hurt themselves or anyone or anything. God can work with that. God can work with that human willfulness and transform it. It could look something like what John Wesley called "Christian perfection." Humans would be filled completely with God's love. Until then, each will be responsible for our own conscious willfulness. Broadening the scope, Lundbom connects this with the previous promises of a united Israel and Judah, as well as a repopulation of people and animals accompanied by a healing of the land. This promise is also something new. The current generation will not suffer as a result of the previous ones. They will deal with their own sin, not the sins of their ancestors whose sin caused the exile.[16]

Verse 31 depicts a promising future: "The days are surely coming, says the LORD, when I will make a new covenant with the house of Israel and the house of Judah." It is a different future than what we can assume is happening when Jeremiah wrote this or the people heard it. It is the word of the LORD. The word "covenant" has a lot of connotations. It is a binding relationship. It has implications of legality, but it is not an arrangement among equals. In this verse, it is a promise of something new—a new agreement, a new arrangement. However, this arrangement is not with the church. The church did not exist in the world at that time. Nor is the arrangement with Babylon or with the other nations or peoples. It is with Israel and Judah together—the descendants of Jacob and their promised land and nation. It must begin with Israel.

This verse gets a lot of attention from commentators. As mentioned above, supersessionism was and remains a means of all sorts of evil perpetrated against the Jews by Christians. American Christians come by it honestly. Calvin wrote, "So we see that this passage refers to the kingdom of Christ, for without Christ the people could not have hoped for anything superior to the law."[17] This is the most egregious of Calvin's theological errors interpreting this book. That his theology was passed along to the Puritans and the colonialism that came with them helps explain some of the "city on a hill," "new Jerusalem" idolatry that fueled and continues to fuel civil religion in America. We are seeing the rottenness of the fruit of this tree currently in 2025. Close to a hundred years before, that it possibly, even probably, led to the Shoah is horrifying.

Modern commentators offer a strong corrective to this important mistake. Stulman makes a succinct corrective and interpretation: "Christian commentators often treat Jeremiah 31:31–34 in complete isolation from its literary and historical setting. It is read as exclusive property of Christians. The new covenant is new

16. Lundbom, *Jeremiah 21–36*, 463.

17. Calvin, *Jeremiah and Lamentations*, 188.

because God initiates the relationship in the face of the people's abject infidelity and recalcitrance."[18] Brueggemann adds,

> Such a supersessionist reading in fact asserts the rejection rather than the reconstitution of Israel, a point not on the horizon of these oracles . . . we are right to posit a deep discontinuity between old and new, but that deep discontinuity is not between Jews and Christians, but between recalcitrant Jews prior to 587 and transformed Jews after 587 who embrace the covenant newly offered by God.[19]

Verse 32 moves again from thinking of the future to considering the past: "It will not be like the covenant that I made with their ancestors when I took them by the hand to bring them out of the land of Egypt—a covenant that they broke, though I was their husband, says the LORD." This verse really takes us back to the very beginning. The Jews were enslaved in Egypt, and the LORD here provides an intimate image of him "taking them by the hand." Verse 32 recalls both the revealing of the LORD and the miraculous work of freeing the people from bondage.

The addition of the phrase, "a covenant they broke," is a reminder of how the exile and destruction occurred. Israel did not keep their end of the promise and are now living with the consequences. The phrase "though I was their husband" is rendered in other translations as "although I was patient with them" (REB). "Master," rather than "husband," is used in the NAB, and this translation is footnoted in NRSV but not in NRSVue. The Tanakh's note says that the meaning of the Hebrew used in the phrase is uncertain, but it uses "espoused" for its English translation.[20] This uncertainty can be read as a mysterious revelation of God: husband, Master, patience, One who adopts. There is implied that the LORD was faithful to the covenant, but this also defends God's character regarding the assumed current reality of exile.

18. Stulman, *Jeremiah*, 273.

19. Brueggemann, *Jeremiah*, 292.

20. Tanakh, 839.

The theology of getting what we deserve holds weight but has limits. Job and, of course, the Shoah push this issue to the point of breaking for some. The end is punctuated with another "Thus says the LORD." This is a revelation from the One. Finally, that word settles the debate. Clements adds, "There is a lot of uncertainty about what new covenant will amount to and how it relates to the law of Moses. One thing for certain, the old covenant has been broken like a dead marriage."[21] Varughese and Modine add that it does not suggest a new Torah, only the covenant is new.[22]

Verse 33 further describes the new covenant: "But this is the covenant that I will make with the house of Israel after those days, says the LORD: I will put my law within them, and I will write it on their hearts, and I will be their God, and they shall be my people." This description of the new covenant is filled with hope. It is the solution, the source of faith for Israel and all peoples. If we can make a leap and substitute "law" for "God's will," which does not eliminate the law but moves it into the reality of irresistible grace, we have a move from God that will lead us to the new heaven and new earth. We are talking about harmony here. It is not that God and the people are identical, but they (we) harmonize. God causes this to happen. And it is beautiful. It is a restoration of husband, master, adopted parent, even friend. We not only know what to do. We desire to do it, and we do it.

Commentators try to shed some light on this vital verse. Lundbom writes, "The new covenant is new because Yahweh's Torah will be written on the human heart. God will need to do this as the human heart 'is deceitful above all things.' Jeremiah 17:9."[23] Stulman adds, "The internalization of the law empowers Israel to love and obey God. It allows Israel to break out of its cycle of failure and fulfill the demands of the covenant."[24] Varughese and Modine have a very Wesleyan view:

21. Clements, *Jeremiah*, 189–90.

22. Varughese and Modine, *Jeremiah 26–52*, 153.

23. Lundbom, *Jeremiah 21–36*, 468–69.

24. Stulman, *Jeremiah*, 273.

> The writing of the law on human hearts clearly implies the gift of a new heart and a new inner disposition and thus the beginning of a new life of obedience and trust in God. . . . It is possible to conclude that obedience in the new covenant relationship is grace initiated and enabled human response to God's offer of newness to those who live in broken relationship with him.[25]

I lack the knowledge to say what "putting my law within them" might mean inside Judaism. Jeremiah would have been familiar with the reform of Josiah. That his calling occurred after that reform testifies to its inadequacy of transformation. Certainly, with the pathways of Orthodox, Conservative, and Reform, there is plenty of disagreement about what it looks like within that faith. Cautiously moving toward applying it within the Methodist Church, this sounds a lot like the gift of the Holy Spirit. This sounds like knowledge of God's will for us and the power to carry it out—and most importantly, the desire to carry it out. It is what Wesley would call "being made perfect in love."[26]

In verse 34, past, present and future meet: "No longer shall they teach one another or say to each other, 'Know the LORD' for they shall all know me, from the least of them to the greatest, says the LORD, for I will forgive their iniquity and remember their sin no more." The past and present involve teaching, advising, empowering to "know the LORD." This promises a future when teachers (and preachers) can retire! At least from the most important teaching of knowing and being in a relationship with the LORD. This is connected to all having this presence, knowledge, willingness written in our hearts.

"From the least of them to the greatest" implies several characteristics. From an economic standpoint, it reflects the notion that "those who have much don't have too much and those that have little do not have too little" (2 Cor 8:15). There is not a promise of sameness. Even in the future, there will be great ones and least ones, but all will know God and have enough to be a part of

25. Varughese and Modine, *Jeremiah 26–52*, 159–61.

26. Wesley, *Plain Account of Christian Perfection*, 1.

the people. This is punctuated with yet another iteration of "saith the LORD." This is a promise directly from God.

Forgiveness is also a vital part of this future. The people, from the greatest to the least, have not kept their part of the covenant. We can try to explain it, blame it on Adam, blame it on the principalities and powers, and a host of truthful explanations. The bottom line is that Israel, humans, and all of creation are out of harmony with the LORD. In this verse, we have a promise of forgiveness and a new relationship with God. It is beyond our comprehension how deep and important this promise is. Jesus tries to help us understand with his parable of the servant who owed the king ten thousand talents—an unpayable debt. And in verse 34, we have a promise that our unpayable debt will be forgiven and remembered no more. Following Jesus's parable, having God's law "written on our hearts" will enable us to do the same for our fellow servants and their one hundred denarii debt (Matt 18:28). Paul believed that God had already fulfilled this part of the promise in the sacrifice of the Son (see 2 Cor 5:19 and most of Paul's writings in some fashion or another). The challenge is among the servants.

This promise opens a tricky question around justice. To push extremes, is it right that both Martin Luther King Jr. and Bull Conner receive full forgiveness? It seems especially unfair given that one seems to have a debt close to one hundred denarii and another close to ten thousand talents. The reality of having "least and greatest" is helpful here. This Protestant interpreter will need to leave that to my Catholic and Orthodox colleagues skilled in purgatorial interpretation. That there are distinct levels of heaven (2 Cor 12:2) may also help sort out the tension between justice and forgiveness. See Dante for more details.

Moving back to life in this world, and possibly the next, commentators add their reflections:

> The knowledge of God is a key piece of Jeremiah's theological construction. In the old world, the knowledge of God was conspicuously absent; neither priest nor people knew Yahweh (2:8, 4:22, 9:3) neither rich nor poor understood the ways of God (5:4, 5). This dearth of

> knowledge led the community down a treacherous road of corruption.[27]

God refuses to leave them there:

> The new covenant offers unqualified forgiveness to broken people who can no longer bear the burden of their guilt . . . forgiveness is more than a characteristic of the new covenant; it is the very basis of the astonishing workings of God. Divine forgiveness makes possible inner transformation, intimacy with God, and an inclusive community that delights in faithful living.[28]

Brueggemann adds, "There will be common, shared access to this knowledge which evidences fundamental egalitarianism in the community . . . all know the story, all accept the sovereignty, and all embrace the commands. All the newness is possible *because* Yahweh has forgiven."[29] The church could learn much here. Is it possible to hold forgiveness in harmony with following Jesus and serving his kingdom as disciples? It is not likely without God's intervention because the harm caused to disciples will compete with capacity to forgive.

In verse 35, underlined with "Thus says the LORD," we have what seems to be a defense of God's power to fulfill these promises. "Thus says the LORD, who gives the sun for light by day and the fixed order of the moon and the stars for light by night, who stirs up the sea so that its waves roar—the LORD of hosts is his name." A key word here is "gift." The sun not only provides light, but it also provides life as we know it. Humans did not create it and will cease to exist without it. It is given to us and to all of creation. From an amateur scientist's point of view, it is interesting that the moon and the waves of the sea are mentioned, as gravity helps form that relationship. More importantly, we created neither, nor have any control over either. God is both giver and has power to make the waves "roar."

27. Stulman, *Jeremiah*, 273.

28. Stulman, *Jeremiah*, 274.

29. Brueggemann, *Jeremiah*, 294.

In the days of the Webb telescope, the belief that God has created and given us the stars is almost beyond comprehension. God promised Abram in Gen 15:5–6 that his descendants will rival the number of stars. This is also a promise of hope that the God who created us will care for us all the way to the end: "The stress on continuity and creation embodies the largest and most comprehensive ground for God's fidelity to Israel imaginable."[30]

Verse 36 is related to verse 35. It reads, "If this fixed order were ever to cease from my presence, says the LORD, then also the offspring of Israel would cease to be a nation before me forever." Only God has power over the sun, moon, stars, and waves. The LORD connects these entities with the existence of the people (nation?) of Israel. This is a difficult promise within Jeremiah. His contemporaries claimed, within the spirit of this promise, that the temple, the Davidic line, and the "nation" (as it was understood 2,500 years ago) could never end. That promise was unconditional. At the time of this verse, all of that was gone. Is this a recommitment? It seems connected with the promises in the rest of the passage. Israel will exist as a people and a nation when the law is written on their hearts.

Verse 37 continues the theme of the previous two and is bookended by "says the LORD." "Thus says the LORD: If the heavens above can be measured and the foundations of the earth below can be explored, then I will reject all the offspring of Israel because of all they have done, says the LORD." This verse is shrouded in mystery; the heavens and earth are both visible and, at least to date, remain mostly unexplored. Forgiveness is implied here again. The sin has not been forgotten yet. But the promise, or re-promise, is that the children of Israel will never be rejected. This is both a statement of their presumed condition in exile and a future promise of continued relationship with the LORD.

We also have another opening to wonder about the measure or degree of heaven and its "levels." Jeremiah "reminds his audience that the one speaking has put the sun, moon, and stars in the heavens . . . if these statutes governing the heavenly bodies depart

30. Brueggemann, *Jeremiah*, 295–96.

from before him, then Israel's seed (continuing as a nation) cease from before him."[31] The problem with this interpretation is that, since the 586 Babylonian exile, Israel has spent little time being a nation, or at least a modern understanding of nation. The Jewish people have continued but in the diaspora. This inconsistency fuels much debate around modern Zionism and the modern nation state of Israel. The divine promise, interpreted by some, is unconditional, but over 2,500 years of history has mostly proven otherwise.[32]

Verse 38 offers a somewhat more practical promise: "The days are surely coming, says the LORD, when the city shall be rebuilt for the LORD from the tower of Hananel to the Corner Gate." Inside this practical promise is also a hope that Jerusalem will once again be the thriving city of David and God's earthly home. The people reading this are asked to hope for this. Once again, adding "says the LORD" underlines the integrity of the promised hope. "The main point of this oracle [vv. 38–40] is that lofty Jerusalem, together with its terraces and surrounding valleys, shall be rebuilt and reconsecrated 'for Yahweh.'"[33] Likewise, Brueggemann notes that "Forever" implies that it is unconditional.[34] Both history and the means used to get to that end invite debate about that interpretation.

Verse 39 continues, "And the measuring line shall go out farther, straight to the hill Gareb, and shall then turn to Goah." The city will not only be rebuilt but will see the "territory enlarged" (1 Chr 4:9–10). Implied is a vision that life will be better post-destruction than it was before. This may also hint at a yet to be realized future when the other promises in the passage come true.

Verse 40 expounds, "The whole valley of the dead bodies and the ashes and all the fields as far as the Wadi Kidron, to the corner of the Horse Gate toward the east, shall be sacred to the LORD. It shall never again be uprooted or overthrown." It is hard to imagine

31. Lundbom, *Jeremiah 21–36*, 487.

32. Brueggemann, *Jeremiah*, 297.

33. Lundbom, *Jeremiah 21–36*, 489.

34. Brueggemann, *Jeremiah*, 299.

this without recalling images from the Shoah. It is a place of death and yet promised to be sacred to the LORD. The loss will not be forgotten but honored. That which was destroyed will become holy. The city will be the home of God. It will be a symbol of God's presence among his redeemed people.[35]

This pericope speaks hope into hopelessness by declaring that the LORD will act in a way not before seen. This promise will be good news for a people who have seen their efforts fail. It is also good news for a people who need to remember that the God of Israel is powerful enough to accomplish all that is written in these verses and in these chapters of consolation. God will make it happen.

DOING SOMETHING NEW

The children of Jacob fell into darkness. Their professions, communities, celebrations, and nation were gone. Babylon, who Jeremiah tells us God used to bring about this catastrophe, will not be far behind. That empire, one of the greatest ever, also fell into darkness. The great Babylonian Emperor Nebuchadnezzar, after one more moment of bragging about how awesome he and his work were, suddenly found himself living in a field eating grass with the oxen (Dan 4:33). In all of this, the people, even the grandiose emperor, continued because God continued. The sovereignty debate ended. Out of the darkness came light. Out of the darkness emerged hope. The details of that for Judah and Israel are explored above in a pericope of Jeremiah's "book of consolation." I am unable to speak to the hope of the Jewish people promised in Jeremiah outside of a possible shared hope with Christians. Hope for Christians living within the boundaries of the United States of America lies with the continued ministry of the Holy Spirit in revealing and expanding the kingdom of God. Our hope is this continuation of the ministry of Jesus. Jesus revealed much of the job description of the Holy Spirit: who will "teach you everything and remind you of all that

35. Fretheim, *Jeremiah*, 165.

I have said to you" (John 14:26b). This is a Christian understanding of having God's law "written on our hearts" or "knowing God from the least to the greatest." The third person of the Trinity has been tasked with completing the mission of the kingdom of a new heaven and new earth with our help. The "our" in this case may be rightly debated and is not meant to be a statement of Christian triumphalism or exclusiveness. However, the baptized and receptors of the Holy Spirit have been called to participate in this work as witnesses.

Christians in America are faced with a time when hope of God's intervention may be all we will have. Whether we draw from Scripture or from secular history, darkness has appeared. Idolatry, violence, and a people who are being formed into the opposite of a people capable of loving God and loving neighbors as ourselves have brought us to this point. But the story continues. It continued for Nebuchadnezzar. It continued, in a way, for a reformed Babylon. And it continued for the people of God known as the children of Abraham, Isaac, and Jacob—the children of the Torah. This chapter, like Jeremiah's chapter 30 through 33, is written in the middle of the destruction, yet envisions hope. My prayer is it will be a witness to the light as all other lights fail.

People are formed. Our formation reveals who and what is forming us. As argued in the first chapter, when capitalism becomes an idol, it forms people into consumers. That becomes our end as well as our means. While this work barely gave a nod to the climate catastrophe unfolding before the world, the fruit of capitalism is consumption of the world. Worship of this idol is death. Hope for the children of Jacob meant returning to the land the one true and sovereign God gave them with a new heart that loved God with all they had. In that new history, God and God's will lives in the people and the land. Some of that hope began with the return of the exiles from Babylon. Some of that hope is yet to be realized.

While Christians must be on guard against supersessionism, we can claim a similar hope through analogy. Our hope is in the kingdom that was born and revealed to us through the Father, Son, and Holy Spirit. We are, for the most part, not Jeremiah's people. As explored in the above exegesis, claiming that Jesus is the one and only "new covenant" Jeremiah predicts is a mistake and one that has led to unimaginable cruelty against the Jews, the greatest so far being the Shoah. Christians have not replaced Jews as God's people. However, Christians can claim that we are a part of the story of Jeremiah and Israel. We are the wild olive branches grafted onto the cultivated tree (Rom 11:17–18). Christians are the sect of Judaism that believes the Messiah has come.[36]

Our hope centers in a recommitment to worship God and God alone. To love God with all our heart, with all our mind, and with all our soul (Matt 22:37). That needs to be written in our hearts. That needs to form us into disciples of Jesus Christ. To follow Jesus and bear witness to that activity is our purpose. His lordship and our response to it is the source and destination of our hope.

Who is the "our" or the "we"? American citizens? "Christian nations"? Humans? "Believers"? The "we" for this essay begins with a group who believe Jesus is Lord and seek to follow him every day. The body of Christ.

Stanley Hauerwas has spent his career calling the church to repentance. While this call encompasses capitalism, Hauerwas's targeted idol is a kind of autonomous freedom that is incompatible with following Jesus and being a part of the church.[37] He is calling the followers of Jesus (whom he calls "church") to see the truth that we are a part of the story of creation, redemption, adventure, and hope. Any other story is an idol. His call is especially that, when we accept as true "that we have no story other than the story we chose when we thought we had no story," we are worshiping the idol of modernity.[38]

36. Hauerwas, lecture in his Christian Ethics course at Duke Divinity School, Louisville, 1992.

37. Myers, "Stanley Hauerwas." Modernity is a consistent theme in Hauerwas's work.

38. Hauerwas, "How Real Is America's Faith?" And, again, throughout his published works and lectures.

Hauerwas's hope is in the truthfulness of the new creation made possible by God, especially the God revealed in Father, Son, and Holy Spirit. In *Approaching the End: Eschatological Reflections on Church, Politics and Life*, Hauerwas begins with a summary of his work: "Theology is an intricate web of *loci* that requires ongoing exploration and repair. Exploration and repair are required because we are tempted to overemphasize one 'doctrine' or *locus* in a manner that distorts what we believe and how we live."[39] In great part, my thesis is trying to explore and refute the "doctrine" that America (and all that comes with it) is the new Israel and is *the* manifestation of the kingdom of God.

Hauerwas's way of understanding theology is compatible with his thinking about narrative. Characters develop and are revealed over time. The plot swerves but eventually unveils and resolves itself in the end. This story, the story of creation, begins and ends with the God who is revealed through Jeremiah and, for Christians, through Jesus. Along that story of exploration and repair, we find hope. And, if I might risk the error of triumphalism, America and the world finds its hope. The end of the story that Jesus is Lord and will reign over a new heaven and new earth.[40] Yet there is also hope for today. There is hope present in the exploration and repair of God's work in the world and especially for those called to participate in that work. We have help.

In their book *The Holy Spirit*, Hauerwas and Will Willimon explore the presence of the third person of the Trinity active in the world today.[41] The Holy Spirit is leading followers (and others) toward the good news of the kingdom of God.[42] The Spirit has taken Jesus' place in the world and is here to remind us of what we already know and to teach us what we are now ready to learn.[43] An

39. Hauerwas, *Sanctify Them in the Truth*, 2, as quoted in Hauerwas, *Approaching the End*, 5.

40. Matt 28:18: "And Jesus came and said to them, 'All authority in heaven and on earth has been given to me,'" and Rev 19 and 21.

41. Hauerwas and Willimon, *Holy Spirit*.

42. Hauerwas and Willimon, *Holy Spirit*, 55.

43. John 14:26.

important exploration and repair is to recognize that Jesus is Lord of all nations and sends his followers to carry the good news to all nations.[44] An essential mark of the good news, of discipleship is the church's catholicity. The Catholic Church is a church formed of individuals in union with God and one another. Unity, at least the unity that comes with the Holy Spirit, is not oppressive uniformity. In order for the Spirit to have room to work, followers of Jesus who are also American citizens especially have some work to do.

We have a powerful beginning with this in the liturgy of baptism. Within the "Baptismal Covenant I" in the *United Methodist Hymnal*, baptism by water is followed immediately with the laying on of hands and a prayer for the Holy Spirit to work within the person being baptized.[45] The new identity of Christian comes with the power of transformation, making us vulnerable to the work of the Holy Spirit. We are given the power to become one as Jesus and the Father are one (John 17:11). Details of some of that work can be found in political scientist Michael Budde's book, *The Borders of Baptism: Identities, Allegiances, and the Church*.[46] Budde writes,

> This book outlines an important concept—what I call "ecclesial solidarity"—that must be reclaimed and deepened if the Christian church is to continue serving the Kingdom of God in our day. By "ecclesial solidarity" I mean the conviction that "being a Christian" is one's primary and formative loyalty, the one that contextualizes and defines the legitimacy of other claimants on allegiance and conscience—those of class, nationality, and state for example.[47]

For Hauerwas, this means that the church needs to be the church so the world can know that it's the world.[48] It means for the church to repent from its idolatry to America, capitalism, and all the violence that comes with worshiping that idol.

44. Matt 28:19
45. *United Methodist Hymnal*, 37.
46. Budde, *Borders of Baptism*.
47. Budde, *Borders of Baptism*, 3.
48. Hauerwas, *Peaceable Kingdom*, 99–104.

Budde's work has a quite simple, yet apparently nearly impossible, call to seek first the kingdom of God.[49] Cavanaugh helps us see the difficulty through his "scale" of idolatry discussed in my first chapter. If Christians living in this country worship America *as* the kingdom of God, Budde's challenge is hard to hear much less live. Sadly, America may all but be destroyed before Christians will see that it is not God. But even here, we have hope. As noted earlier, God's people have been through this before. Nations come and go. Empires and the smaller nations they usually leave behind come and go. The kingdom of God that is hope for all peoples and nations (Rev 7:9) is where the story is heading. And for those who weep for the love of America, Budde brings another word of hope from Origen: "Just by being what God wants it to be, the Church contributes to the world around it; and it need not serve the empire on the empire's terms in order to act 'responsibly.'"[50]

Christians in America live within and are partially formed by America. Perhaps one way to think about this is to ask if we are Christians who happen to be living in America, or are we Americans who happen to be Christians? To even ask that question gets to much of what I am trying to do in this thesis. For example, I am currently leading one of my congregations to begin a friendship with our three local schools. In some particularly important ways, these schools represent the empire. From children, including Christians, being led to pledge allegiance to America to indoctrination in what might be called a Niebuhrian world view, where Christianity and America are generally compatible, public schools offer indoctrination into the "American life."[51] This indoctrination includes allegiance to the constitution, support of democracy, support of capitalism, and a deep understanding that violence is justified to defend these and other allegiances. While public education does or can do much more than that, they at least do that. The citizens formed by public schools also are our neighbors whom Jesus told us to love. This new friendship has found me shopping

49. Budde, *Borders of Baptism*, 10.

50. Budde, *Borders of Baptism*, 18.

51. See Niebuhr and Heimert, *Nation So Conceived*, among others.

for women's underwear (to include in care packages) at the local Walmart. I even had to ask for help! It is one of the acts of mercy to which Jesus specifically called us. "You saw me naked and clothed me."[52] Seeking the kingdom first requires humility. Our hope is that by seeking the kingdom first (another way of saying loving God with all we have), we open ourselves to the promise of God's love and healing for the nations in Rev 22:2. In some form or another, there is hope for America. The followers of Jesus may help that by discerning and changing the allegiances that they honor first.

This might also open Christians to a new adventurous chapter in our story. Budde suggests, especially as the church has mostly moved into the global south, that the future of Christianity will be formed by Catholicism and Pentecostalism. Whatever church that produces will likely not be boring. As a United Methodist leader, I am encouraged by this trend. From the beginning, Wesley helped build bridges, and it is in the United Methodist tradition to be a part of both the Roman Catholic and Pentecostal communities.[53]

In 1990, I spent a week in Esquipulas, Nicaragua, working for Habitat for Humanity. Our group went to Mass in the morning and to a Pentecostal service that evening. Before Mass, the American priest came to our pew and invited us to the Eucharist: "Rome has said we are not supposed to serve Protestants, but we are a long way from Rome. Thank you for helping our community." (Sadly, I was the only one from our group who went forward to receive. The bridge needs repairing on both sides.) The Pentecostal service that evening was wild. The band, with a very memorable leader, played and led the singing for an hour. Then the pastor preached for an hour. As we were leaving, the pastor thanked us for our work and for coming to worship. "Most of the work teams walk by and look at us like we are crazy." Both services, as different as could be, were packed inside with those looking into the open windows as well. Given the attendance I have seen for the churches I have pastored, that Christians living in America have been set aside as "better" or "first" lacks evidence.

52. Matt 25:36.

53. Bevins, "Wesley and the Pentecostals."

The hospitality of the Nicaraguan people was especially outstanding considering the multi-year, illegal war the United States had fought against the democratically elected government. I toured a hospital and home for children who were fitted with artificial limbs blown off by land mines paid for with my tax dollars. They did not need to lecture or hate; they simply showed us the results. The claim I have always heard of America being a "Christian nation" requires further interrogation.

Hauerwas and Budde share a common call for the church to renounce violence. This call strikes at the heart of the idol. Violence is fruit from the tree of capitalism. This idol also tempts Christians to try and live in a way that bears witness to the ultimacy of death.

Hauerwas, using the work of John Howard Yoder, opens us to a revelation of God and what following God, revealed in Jesus, says about our "self-defense" and Christian complicity with war. Hauerwas writes, "Pacifism, according to Yoder, is required by the cross of Christ, for it is in the cross that God refuses to save coercively. Jesus therefore does not fit the Kantian mold, because he is not commending his ethic for just anyone, but for those who would be his disciples."[54]

The hard truth is Christians are not like everyone else. Trying to make ourselves like everyone else or to make following Jesus a "rational" choice has helped get us where we are, especially in America.[55] Christians are called to follow Jesus no matter what, with no exception for "justified" violence. I write this in the spirit of "exploration and repair," as I have been told it is a lot easier for a white, middle-class, American male to hold a strong position on nonviolence than perhaps for any other group in the world. However, could we just start with my "group"? If all white, middle-class, American men who are trying to follow Jesus sold our guns, that would be a great start. I wonder about a comparison with the fictional characters portrayed by John Wayne and James Arness with Jesus and the communion of the saints that have followed him since. We might see how much is created by an idealized,

54. Hauerwas, *Approaching the End*, 135.

55. Hauerwas, *Approaching the End*, 135.

beautiful demonstration of violence that is delusional. Guns are a symbol and an attempt at defeating death. In reality, they are instruments and symbols of fear. How can we follow Jesus and be so afraid of death? Our end is not survival but abundant life.[56] "We were created to be creatures whose end *telos* (purpose) and end (destination) is God."[57]

Throughout the New Testament, we are told that death has been defeated, and God's eternal life is where all things are heading. Jeremiah hints at that for his people in what are arguably God's unconditional promises to be with them, the land, and Jerusalem "forever."[58] Part of getting there may be watching God run wild a bit. Budde quotes Shenk about Pentecostalism: "The starting point is not rational discourse about the person and work of the Spirit but direct personal encounter with the Holy Spirit and the release of the charismata of the Spirit into the life of the believers."[59] For aspects of American culture and many in the pews where I pastor (whose saviors include Rooster Cogburn, Matt Dillon, James Bond, and a host of fictional heroes for whom violence is a means), the abandonment of Christian participation in and support of violence is beyond rational discourse. It will take a direct conversion and personal encounter with the Holy Spirit for there to be a change. Willimon and Hauerwas bring in Scripture to this shift: "The Acts of the Apostles is the story of how, under the guidance of the Holy Spirit, the Church was given the mission to be a showcase that the violence inherent in our babbling isolation from one another has been overwhelmed by the cross and resurrection of Christ."[60]

What sort of people does God need—people who would be more willing to die than to kill? How would such a people be formed? And for what purpose? One path to becoming such a person is to grow from belief to becoming. Christians need to

56. John 10:10b.

57. Hauerwas and Willimon, *Holy Spirit*, 86.

58. Jer 31:36.

59. Budde, *Borders of Baptism*, 29.

60. Hauerwas and Willimon, *Holy Spirit*, 36.

be formed into disciples. Karl Barth wrote, "For in Jesus Christ God has created all things. He has created all of us. We exist not apart from Him, whether we are aware of it or not; and the whole cosmos exists not apart from Him, but in Him, borne by Him, the Almighty Word. To know Him is to know all."[61] As Christians live into that, what may seem rationally impossible becomes almost irrelevant. Where this belief is needed is in the church. Too often, claims to primacy of Christ has led to coercion and self-substantiation. If used to build Christian character, however, we can hear the words "what have I to dread, what have I to fear" with new ears.[62] We must always remain teachable.[63]

Hauerwas has left us a trail to follow. Beginning with Aristotle through Aquinas, then to Barth and Yoder, he highlights the importance of acquiring virtue as vital to following Jesus and bearing witness to the kingdom of God. While much of my thesis has discussed what happens when Christians either fail to acquire virtue or do not see its value in discipleship. The combination of virtuous habits alongside the daily discipline of inviting the Holy Spirit to remind us of what we already know and teach us what we are now ready to learn (John 14:26) could provide a pathway toward what Jeremiah is envisioning with "hearts that know God" (31:34).

Hauerwas discusses in the chapter the importance as well as a means of acquiring the virtues necessary to be a faithful witness to hope. He begins with the obvious: "It is, therefore, never a question whether we will or will not develop habits and virtues, but what kinds of habits we will develop."[64] The habit of watching cable news for hours a day will form a different Christian from one who reads Scripture and prays hours a day.

More is needed. For those familiar with his work, Hauerwas is never far from laying brick, and that activity requires not only

61. Karl Barth, *Dogmatics in Outline*, 26, as quoted in Hauerwas, *With the Grain*, 162.

62. Hoffman, "Leaning on the Everlasting Arms," 133.

63. Hauerwas, *With the Grain*, 174.

64. Hauerwas, *With the Grain*, 161.

habit but training, practice, and a commitment to excellence. Recently, I heard a witness of a congregation that has started meeting in the middle of the week to read Scripture together. Combining personal reading with the discernment of part of the body of Christ is learning to lay brick well. To trade that for another installment of the story told by the media is a source of hope. "Just as we learn a craft by repeatedly producing the same product that was produced when we were first learning the craft, so we become virtuous by performing actions that are virtuous."[65]

These calls to a rehabilitation are underlined in Hauerwas and Willimon's book *The Holy Spirit*:

> Holiness demands that whatever else may be said about the work of the Holy Spirit, at the very least what must be said is that who God is and what God does matters. The proper task of truly *Christian* ethics is to display how the Holy Spirit makes a difference for Christian living.[66]

A turn to hope is also a call to Christians to re-habituate ourselves, to discipline ourselves, into a people who live into the hope God is calling the new heaven and new earth—the hope of the kingdom of God. As those habits are acquired, reacquired, formed and reformed (regular worship attendance, individual and corporate Scripture reading and study, participation in the Eucharist, service to the congregation and neighborhood are great places to start or recommit), we move toward our most vital task in participating in the hope God brings to the church, the nations, and to all of creation: witness.

What that witness will look like is both a church and preacher fight. This thesis is offering the importance to witnessing that God is sovereign over the nations, including but not limited to America. Borrowing from Kavin Rowe,

> You don't have to wait long in Acts before being introduced to Luke's programmatic thesis: after they have received "the power of the Holy Spirit" the risen Jesus

65. Hauerwas, *With the Grain*, 161.

66. Hauerwas and Willimon, *Holy Spirit*, 67.

> tells them they "shall be my witnesses in Jerusalem and in all Judea and Samaria to the end of the earth" (Acts 1:8). Such a mission is required because the disciples were to make known to the world that Jesus, not Caesar, was Lord.[67]

This is a much different witness than telling people that Jesus died for our sins and if we believe that we get to go to heaven when we die and if we do not, we go to hell. That witness has abandoned not only the importance of acquiring and habituating virtues as disciples of Jesus, but it abandons the practices of loving God and loving neighbor as yourself.

That love is the source of hope for all things, and it requires witnesses in a world where love is conditional—love that does not worship God as sovereign. In the words of Stanley Hauerwas,

> If we and the world existed by necessity, then no witness, no story of creation, would be required. But God did not have to create, much less redeem; yet we have it on good authority that God has created and redeemed. Creation and redemption constitute the story necessary for us to know who we are. Such knowledge comes only through the telling of this story.[68]

This is the task before the church today. We are to tell the story of hope. Perhaps better said, we are to live the story of hope. Our practice of virtue increases our storytelling and story-living skills. The importance of our acceptance of this task cannot be underestimated. The previous chapter, as dark as it is with the people losing all that they thought God would never allow them to lose, is not an exaggeration. It is happening in real time. The power of the principalities is not bashful about giving its witness. The church, in all its different forms and ways—congregations, denominations, Catholic, Protestant, and anyone else claiming Jesus—must find the courage of witness. The specifics of that witness will be shaped by the leading of the Holy Spirit. Witness is why we exist, and that

67. C. Kavin Rowe, *World Upside Down: Reading Acts in the Graeco-Roman Age*, 120, as quoted in Hauerwas and Willimon, *Holy Spirit*, 51.

68. Hauerwas, *With the Grain*, 207.

is where we will find our hope and share the light of that hope into the darkness. The darkness will not overcome it.[69]

The final word of hope is that Christians know how the story ends. Life is not just one thing after another, nor is it a slow or fast ride into the abyss. Those called by God to be a people, both Jew and gentile, have seen plenty of abysses. However, here we still are. The end of the story is life. Through the birth, life, death, resurrection, and ascension of Jesus, God has made a new heaven and a new earth. Right now, we can only see that as a reflection, but at the right time, we will see clearly.[70]

GOD IS NOT FINISHED: A SERMON AND FINAL REFLECTIONS ON JEREMIAH 31:23–40

Jeremiah's words have been tearing things apart in three straight sermons—idolatry leading to violence leading to death. However, just when things are at their worst, just when Jerusalem and Solomon's temple are about to be, or have already been destroyed, God tells Jeremiah to say this:

> Thus says the LORD of hosts, the God of Israel: Once more they shall use these words in the land of Judah and in its towns when I restore their fortunes: "The LORD bless you, O abode of righteousness, O holy hill!" And Judah and all its towns shall live there together, and the farmers and those who wander with their flocks. I will satisfy the weary, and all who are faint I will replenish. (31:23–25)

Death and all that led up to it does not have the final word. The final word is that God has declared life, and all that comes with it, especially the land and Jerusalem, will be rebuilt. Jeremiah was told to speak this word of hope. And we know from Ezra and Nehemiah that this happened. The people returned from exile. The

69. John 1:5.

70. 1 Cor 13:12.

city (and we assume the towns and society) and the temple were rebuilt.

There is more. The farmers and shepherds will return. The weary and the faint, God will strengthen and satisfy. All who lost or are about to lose hear these words. It is not over. There is hope.

As the passage and vision unfolds, we begin to see something new. God will behave differently toward the people. God will sow seed. Both people and animals will multiply in the same land where the LORD had plucked up and broken down. Just where God overthrew, destroyed, and brought evil, so God will watch over them to build and to plant. This hope is a vision of something new—a new life and new help from the LORD. It will also be a new relationship with those who are being sown at that time. They will not be trapped in having to suffer or to repeat what had been taught and shown to them. The breaking of the old covenant was the reason behind the destruction of the nation. Being rescued from slavery in Egypt, the children of Israel agreed to be a people formed by the Torah, by the law God gave Moses. They failed completely. But now there is a new covenant. The new covenant will be written on the heart. It will be written on everyone's heart. The new covenant will not be something the people must do. It will be something people want to do. Our hearts will long for God. Of course we will love God with all we have. Thy will, not ours, be done.

Christians have made some serious theological errors that have led to conclusions like the notion that we have replaced the Jews as God's people. Even worse, we have blamed the Jewish people for killing Jesus, unleashing horrors upon them, including the Holocaust. One of those serious errors is to believe Jeremiah is predicting the coming of Jesus in his pronouncement of the new covenant. While we have some proof texting in Hebrews to come to that conclusion, especially in chapter 8, where Jesus is the mediator of "a better covenant" (v. 6), when we read and study all of Hebrews (especially chapter 11), we know this is a serious error. So, we must say, the new covenant God promises through Jeremiah has to do with the exiles returning to the land and rebuilding that which God allowed to be destroyed. As to the law being written on the heart, that is both here and yet to come, in that we have witnesses whose lives reflected a changed heart alongside those who are still waiting. But we can grab hope from this passage. What would it be like to have God's will written on our hearts? What would it be like to see the church and, perhaps, even America restored? What would it be like to have hope again?

That has indeed been promised to us, the followers of Jesus. But much like our Jewish kin, we are also called to something new. We are called to have God in our hearts as a witness of the kingdom of Jesus Christ. That will require a reshaping of hearts that are still captivated by death. We have hearts that fear an end that God has promised will not come. Where would we start in asking God to help us? We must renew our love for God with everything we have—mind, body, soul. And we must see everyone we meet as an eternal neighbor, or at least as someone who could be so for us someday. The false gods of nationalism and consumerism must be burned up. Our understanding that violence is God's will must be offered up for transformation. We must learn to love God more than country and our stuff, or the worship of buying stuff. This needs to happen from the least to the greatest. But it can begin with us.

Stanley Hauerwas says we are formed by habits. We can be formed by faithful habits leading us toward hope, or we can be formed by unfaithful habits that will continue to keep us trapped in the hopelessness we are either now in or that awaits us.

The good news in Jeremiah and for us is that God will do this! In the story of the Jewish people, as well as the story of the church, God does not seem to be in a hurry. It is a daily project of reforming our hearts, of reforming our habits, so that we become living witnesses of God's will being done on earth as it is in heaven. That day-to-day project is where we find hope. God will do this and chooses to do it with us.

There is a hard way or an easy way, but God will have a people formed by this newness of heart. We have opportunities to practice this every day. Many in my congregation have heard my confessions of getting lost on TV or the internet. Doing that right before bedtime also affects my sleep. Last night, I shut them all off and read Scripture. That is some movement toward this new covenant.

Michael Cartwright said his congregation decided to start meeting in the middle of the week to read Scripture together instead of spending the evening getting lost. They are finding hope there. There is nothing holding us back from doing that here. That, too, would be a witness to a new people offering ourselves up to this new thing God is calling us to do and be. It will be different for different groups and churches, just like it will be different for Jews and Christians. But it is the same God who is making these promises and making this happen.

Is it possible to imagine a world without America? For Christians, are we willing to imagine it *if* it led to the growth of the kingdom of God? What is argued above is meant to bring the question *and* help us realize it doesn't matter if we ask it or not. Throughout Jeremiah, God asserts sovereignty over the nations. Babylon is useful for a while, then it ends. Even God's chosen, the remnant in Judah, will stop for a while. Will it help Christian discipleship if we surrender to God's sovereignty over the nations, including America?

Finally, we know how the story ends. Thanks to the birth, life, death, resurrection, and ascension of Jesus, thanks to Jeremiah, thanks to the Holy Spirit, who is here right now reminding us of what we have learned and teaching us what we are now ready to learn, we have hope that we will see God's new heaven and new earth. God's new city. God's new life. Amen.

Bibliography

Baker, Kelly J. *The Gospel According to the Klan: The KKK's Appeal to Protestant America, 1915–1930*. Lawrence, KS: University Press of Kansas, 2018.

Berrigan, Daniel. *Jeremiah: The World, the Wound of God*. Minneapolis: Fortress, 1999.

Bevins, Winfield H. "Wesley and the Pentecostals." *The Pneuma Review*, July 10, 2006. http://pneumareview.com/wesley-and-the-pentecostals/.

Bracke, John M. *Jeremiah 30–52 and Lamentations*. Louisville: Westminster John Knox, 2000.

Bright, John. *Jeremiah*. Anchor Bible 21. New York: Doubleday, 1990.

Brueggemann, Walter. *A Commentary on Jeremiah: Exile and Homecoming*. Grand Rapids: Eerdmans, 1997.

———. *Theology of the Old Testament: Testimony, Dispute, Advocacy*. Minneapolis: Fortress, 2012.

———. *To Build, to Plant: A Commentary on Jeremiah 26–52*. Grand Rapids: Eerdmans, 1991.

Budde, Michael L. *The Borders of Baptism: Identities, Allegiances, and the Church*. Eugene, OR: Cascade, 2011.

———. *Foolishness to Gentiles: Essays on Empire, Nationalism, and Discipleship*. Eugene, OR: Cascade, 2022.

Calvin, John. *Jeremiah and Lamentations*. The Crossway Classic Commentaries, edited by Alister McGrath and J. I. Packer. Wheaton, IL: Crossway, 2000.

Camp, Lee C. "The Christian Imagination: Willie James Jennings." No Small Endeavor with Lee C. Camp, Oct. 29, 2020. https://www.nosmallendeavor.com/the-christian-imagination-willie-james-jennings.

Cavanaugh, William. *The Uses of Idolatry*. Oxford: Oxford University Press, 2024. Kindle ed.

Clements, Ronald E. *Jeremiah*. Interpretation: A Bible Commentary for Teaching and Preaching. Louisville: John Knox, 1988.

The Complete Parallel Bible with the Old and New Testaments with the Apocryphal/Deuterocanonical Books: New Revised Standard Version, Revised English Bible, New American Bible, New Jerusalem Bible. Oxford: Oxford University Press, 1993.

Creach, Jerome. *Violence in Scripture*. Louisville: Westminster John Knox, 2013.

Fretheim, Terence E. *Jeremiah*. Macon, GA: Smyth & Helwys, 2002.

Gentry, Dana. "'Very Strange Similarities' but No Link Yet Between Las Vegas Bombing, New Orleans Terror Attack." *Louisiana Illuminator*, Jan. 2, 2025. https://lailluminator.com/2025/01/02/las-vegas-cybertruck/.

Halper, Katie. "'Why I Quit the State Department Over Gaza' with Josh Paul and Jen Perelman." The Katie Halper Show, Aug. 13, 2024. https://www.youtube.com/watch?v=MZ9BnzVRd_4.

Hauerwas, Stanley. *Approaching the End: Eschatological Reflection on Church, Politics and Life*. Grand Rapids: Eerdmans, 2014.

———. "How Real Is America's Faith?" *The Guardian*, Oct. 16, 2010. https://www.theguardian.com/commentisfree/belief/2010/oct/16/faith-america-secular-britain.

———. *The Peaceable Kingdom: A Primer in Christian Ethics*. South Bend, IN: University of Notre Dame Press, 1983.

———. *War and the American Difference*. Ada, MI: Baker Academic, 2011.

———. *With the Grain of the Universe: The Church's Witness and Natural Theology*. Grand Rapids: Brazos, 2002.

Hauerwas, Stanley, and William H. Willimon. *The Holy Spirit*. Nashville: Abingdon, 2015.

Hedges, Chris. *America: The Farewell Tour*. New York: Simon & Schuster, 2018.

Hill, John. *Friend or Foe? The Figure of Babylon in the Book of Jeremiah MT*. Leiden: Brill, 1999.

Hoffman, Elisha. "Leaning on the Everlasting Arms." Music by Anthony Showalter. *The United Methodist Hymnal*. Nashville: The United Methodist Publishing House, 1989.

Holladay, William L. *Jeremiah 1: A Commentary on the Book of the Prophet Jeremiah Chapters 1–25*. Minneapolis: Fortress, 1986.

Holladay, William L., and Paul D. Hanson. *Jeremiah 2: A Commentary on the Book of the Prophet Jeremiah, Chapters 26–52*. Minneapolis: Fortress, 1989. https://muse.jhu.edu/book/45966.

Jennings, Willie James. *The Christian Imagination: Theology and the Origins of Race*. New Haven, CT: Yale University Press, 2010.

———. "Willie James Jennings Workshops on the Christian Imagination at BYU." BYU Religious Education, Dec. 30, 2020. https://www.youtube.com/watch?v=IaKUGoE65vs&t=1955s.

Keefe, Patrick Radden. *Empire of Pain: The Secret History of the Sackler Dynasty*. New York: Doubleday, 2021.

Kessler, Glenn, et al. "Trump's False or Misleading Claims Total 30,573 Over Four Years." *Washington Post*, Jan. 24, 2021. https://www.washingtonpost.com/politics/2021/01/24/trumps-false-or-misleading-claims-total-30573-over-four-years/.

Kent, Ana Hernández. "The State of U.S. Household Wealth." Federal Reserve Bank of St. Louis, July 23, 2025. https://www.stlouisfed.org/open-vault/2025/june/the-state-of-us-household-wealth/.

Lu, Marcus. "Visualizing Wealth Distribution in America (1990–2023)." Visual Capitalist, Feb. 19, 2024. https://www.visualcapitalist.com/wealth-distribution-in-america/.

Lundbom, Jack R. *Jeremiah 1–20: A New Translation with Introduction and Commentary*. Anchor Yale Bible 21A. New Haven, CT: Yale University Press, 2021.

———. *Jeremiah 21–36: A New Translation with Introduction and Commentary*. Anchor Yale Bible 21B. New Haven, CT: Yale University Press, 2021.

———. *Jeremiah 37–52: A New Translation with Introduction and Commentary*. Anchor Yale Bible 21C. New Haven, CT: Yale University Press, 2021.

Lundbom, Jack R., et al., eds. *The Book of Jeremiah: Composition, Reception and Interpretation*. Leiden: Brill, 2018.

McCarraher, Eugene. *The Enchantments of Mammon: How Capitalism Became the Religion of Modernity*. Cambridge, MA: Harvard University Press, 2019.

Miller, Patrick. "The Book of Jeremiah: Introduction, Commentary, and Reflections." New Interpreter's Bible Commentary 6, edited by Leander E. Keck, 462–917. Nashville: Abingdon, 2001.

Moore, Joe, and Jon Land. *White Robes and Broken Badges: Infiltrating the KKK and Exposing the Evil Among Us*. New York: Harper, 2024.

Myers, Ken. "Stanley Hauerwas on the Modern Idea of Freedom." Mars Hill Audio, Sept. 5, 2013. https://mha-members.org/atanley-hauerwas-on-the-modern-idea-of-freedom/.

Niebuhr, Reinhold, and Alan Heimert. *A Nation So Conceived: Reflections on the History of America from Its Early Visions to Its Present Power*. New York: Charles Scribner's Sons, 1963.

Oord, Christian. "Believe It or Not: Since Its Birth the USA Has Only Had 17 Years of Peace." War History Online, Mar. 19, 2019. https://www.warhistoryonline.com/instant-articles/usa-only-17-years-of-peace.html.

Rowe, C. Kavin. *World Upside Down: Reading Acts in the Graeco-Roman Age*. Oxford: Oxford University Press, 2009.

Rush. *2112*. Chicago: Mercury Records, 1976.

Sherman, Arloc, et al. "A Guide to Statistics on Historical Trends in Income Inequality." Center on Budget and Policy Priorities, Dec. 11, 2024. https://www.cbpp.org/research/poverty-and-inequality/a-guide-to-statistics-on-historical-trends-in-income-inequality.

Stringfellow, William. *Conscience and Obedience: The Politics of Romans 13 and Revelation 13 in Light of the Second Coming*. Eugene, OR: Wipf & Stock, 2004.

———. *An Ethic for Christians and Other Aliens in a Strange Land*. Eugene, OR: Wipf & Stock, 2004.

Stulman, Louis. *Jeremiah*. Abingdon Old Testament Commentaries. Nashville: Abingdon, 2005.

Stulman, Louis, and Edward Silver. *The Oxford Handbook of Jeremiah*. Oxford: Oxford University Press, 2021.

United Methodist Hymnal. Nashville: The United Methodist Publishing House, 1989.

United Nations. "Climate Reports." https://www.un.org/en/climatechange/.

Varughese, Alex, and Mitchel Modine. *Jeremiah 26–52: A Commentary in the Wesleyan Tradition*. Kansas City: Beacon Hill, 2010.

Wesley, John. *A Plain Account of Christian Perfection*. Kansas City: Beacon Hill, 1966.

www.ingramcontent.com/pod-product-compliance
Lightning Source LLC
LaVergne TN
LVHW020638100826
845148LV00012B/2239

* 9 7 9 8 3 8 5 2 6 0 8 7 4 *